AARP
iPad®
tech to connect

by Barbara Boyd

WILEY

John Wiley & Sons, Inc.

AARP iPad®: Tech to Connect

Published by
John Wiley & Sons, Inc.
111 River Street
Hoboken, NJ 07030-5774

www.wiley.com

Copyright © 2012 by John Wiley & Sons, Inc., Hoboken, New Jersey

Published by John Wiley & Sons, Inc., Hoboken, New Jersey

Published simultaneously in Canada

For general information on our other products and services, please contact our Customer Care Department within the U.S. at 877-762-2974, outside the U.S. at 317-572-3993, or fax 317-572-4002.

For technical support, please visit www.wiley.com/techsupport.

This and other AARP books are available in print and e-formats at AARP's online bookstore, aarp.org/bookstore.

Wiley publishes in a variety of print and electronic formats and by print-on-demand. Some material included with standard print versions of this book may not be included in e-books or in print-on-demand. If this book refers to media such as a CD or DVD that is not included in the version you purchased, you may download this material at http://booksupport.wiley.com. For more information about Wiley products, visit www.wiley.com.

Cataloging in Publication information is available from the Publisher

ISBN: 978-1-118-38796-2 (pbk); 978-1-118-45993-5 (ebk); 978-1-118-45899-0 (ebk); 978-1-118-45898-3 (ebk)

Manufactured in the United States of America

10 9 8 7 6 5 4 3 2 1

WILEY

Have fun and connect

Unlike your kids and grandkids, you probably didn't grow up glued to high-tech gadgets. You might even still be using that bulky computer on your desk. Now there's another option: your iPad. Those light, portable computers give you the freedom to plug in wherever you are.

If you're feeling overwhelmed by your choices, or intimidated by the new technology, maybe you need a little help getting acquainted with the ins and outs. This book is for you.

Dedicated to helping you stay connected with your friends, family, and community and stretch your money, AARP has joined with Dummies to offer this how-to guide.

This easy-to-understand resource offers

- An introduction to using your iPad physically (how and what to tap, swipe, and pinch) and otherwise (as a web browser, a phone, or a video camera)
- Step-by-step instructions for doing everything from downloading apps and free e-books to connecting with Wi-Fi networks
- Ways to protect your security

So come on board. Let us be your guide.

AARP is a nonprofit, nonpartisan membership organization that helps people 50 and older improve their lives. For more than 50 years, AARP has been serving our members and society by creating positive social change. AARP's mission is to enhance the quality of life for all as we age; lead positive social change; and deliver value to members through information, service and advocacy.

About the Author

Barbara Boyd writes about food, gardens, travel, and technology. She's written for *ChilePepper Magazine, Islands,* and *BeeCulture*. With Joe Hutsko, she co-wrote *iPhone 4S All-in-One For Dummies* and the third edition of *Macs All-in-One For Dummies*. *AARP iPad: Tech To Connect* is Barbara's third book written for John Wiley and Sons, Inc., and her first for the AARP Tech To Connect series.

Barbara worked at Apple from 1985 to 1990, beginning as a network administrator for the executive staff. She then took a position as an administrator in the technical product support group. Barbara recalls working with people who went on to become top names in technology — it was an exciting time to be in Silicon Valley and at Apple in particular. That experience instilled a lifelong fascination with technology and Apple products. Her interest and experience led to subsequent jobs in marketing and publishing at IDG (International Data Group) and later for a small San Francisco design firm. In 1998, she left the corporate world to study Italian, write, and teach.

Presently, Barbara stays busy writing, keeping up with technology, growing olives, and beekeeping. (She's a certified honey taster.) Her next writing project will be a memoir of building a farm and house in Italy. Barbara divides her time between city life in Rome and country life on an olive farm in Calabria, which she blogs about at www.honeybeesandolivetrees.blogspot.com/.

Dedication

I dedicate this book to my adorable husband, Ugo de Paula. I can never thank him enough for his patience and support. Everything seems to fall by the wayside when I'm writing, and he not only never complains but he picks up the slack — a marriage that's an equal partnership is a lovely thing. Ti amo tesoronemio.

Author's Acknowledgments

After writing several books I've learned that the author's name on the cover represents a fraction of the people who contribute to the final product. Many warm thanks go to Bob Woerner at Wiley for asking me to write this book. I couldn't have had a better project editor than Tonya Cupp, whose experience and tight editing certainly made me look better as a writer. Thanks also go to technical editor Dennis R. Cohen, who provided spot-on edits and corrections. As always, I like to thank the anonymous people at Wiley who contributed to this book — not just editorial, but tech support, legal, accounting, and even the person who delivers the mail. I don't know you but I appreciate the job you do; it takes a lot of worker bees to keep the hive healthy, and each task is important to the whole.

Thanks to my agent, Carole Jelen, who looks out for me, and to my dear friend, Joe Hutsko, who got me started in the tech writing business. Lastly, thanks to my cousin, Heather Funk, for her willingness to participate in the FaceTime phone calls for the figures (take after take after take) and pitching in as photograper for the photo of the iPad SIM card tray.

And of course, thanks to you, dear reader, for opening this book. Whether you bought it or received it as a gift, I appreciate your support and interest.

Publisher's Acknowledgments

We're proud of this book; please send us your comments at http://dummies.custhelp.com. For other comments, please contact our Customer Care Department within the U.S. at 877-762-2974, outside the U.S. at 317-572-3993, or fax 317-572-4002.

Some of the people who helped bring this book to market include the following:

Acquisitions and Editorial

Project Editor: Tonya Maddox Cupp

Executive Editor: Bob Woerner

Technical Editor: Dennis R. Cohen

Editorial Manager: Jodi Jensen

Editorial Assistant: Leslie Saxman

Sr. Editorial Assistant: Cherie Case

Cover Photo: ©Dougal Waters/Digital Vision/ Jupiter Images

Composition Services

Project Coordinator: Sheree Montgomery

Layout and Graphics: Christin Swinford

Proofreaders: John Greenough, Melanie Hoffman

Indexer: BIM Indexing & Proofreading Services

Publishing and Editorial for Technology Dummies

Richard Swadley, Vice President and Executive Group Publisher

Andy Cummings, Vice President and Publisher

Mary Bednarek, Executive Acquisitions Director

Mary C. Corder, Editorial Director

Publishing for Consumer Dummies

Kathleen Nebenhaus, Vice President and Executive Publisher

Composition Services

Debbie Stailey, Director of Composition Services

Table of Contents

Introduction

Apple products are known for their simple, intuitive user-interface. Nonetheless, for someone who isn't a full-fledged techie, using an electronic device can be (at best) intimidating or (at worst) downright frustrating. That's where this book comes in. Whether you bought your iPad or received it as a well-intentioned gift, this book shows you how to use your iPad from the moment you take it out of the box. This book mainly applies to later iPad versions.

About This Book

This book includes *everything* you need to know to get started and get comfortable with your iPad. It does have lots of starting points and can lead to well-rounded use of your new device. My goal is to provide instructions for the most basic iPad functions along with some of the more interesting or advanced ones, too. After reading this book, I want you to be familiar with the iPad. I'd like you to reach a comfort level that encourages you to try things on your own. You'll find that iPad basics apply to most iPad apps, even if the apps have a completely different purpose. For example, when you learn how to type and edit text in a Mail message, those same skills apply when you type a note in Notes or an address in Contacts. If you dictate in one app, you'll probably find it useful in other apps as well.

Conventions

To help you understand how the book is laid out, I use a couple of style conventions. Each chapter is broken down into tasks. Each task provides step-by-step instructions that you follow to complete the task. Where a step might not be 100-percent clear with words alone, I've included a figure to show you what you should see on your iPad.

Sidebars are in-depth explanations of functions that are interesting but, again, not necessary. You may find the sidebar makes more sense after you do the task at hand a few times.

 Sometimes you'll see a Tech Tip icon, like the one you see here, next to a paragraph. That means I think this information might save you some time or effort somewhere along the way.

Who This Book Is For

The person most likely to benefit from this book is someone who needs a quick, step-by-step introduction to the iPad. Most of the instructions are for people who are using the iPad on its own, without connecting to a desktop computer. Whether you have a limited technical background or are already somewhat knowledgeable, you can get comfortable and discover something new to do with your device.

How This Book Is Organized

This book is divided into 14 chapters and each chapter is divided into tasks. If you're unfamiliar with the iPad, I recommend reading the first three chapters, which lead you through taking your iPad out of the box, setting up an Apple ID and e-mail account, and mastering the gestures you use to control the touch screen.

Each chapter tells you about one app or several related apps. I put the apps that I think you will find most important toward the front of the book — apps that help you stay in touch with people through e-mail, messages, and video chats. Chapter 6 gets you on the web so you can discover new things or research something specific. Subsequent chapters cover the Maps and Camera apps. The Calendar and Clock apps have surprisingly helpful uses, as does the Notes app. The chapters toward the end of the book focus on using your iPad as an entertainment source for reading e-books, listening to music, or watching videos. The last chapter offers tips on troubleshooting. Should you have a problem with your iPad, you can follow the steps to attempt to fix a problem before returning to the Apple store or contacting Apple technical support. Online at `http://www.wiley.com/go/ipadtechtoconnect`, you will find a bonus chapter titled "Securing Your Data andiPad."

If you have comments or questions about this book, I'm happy to hear from you. Anything you say helps me write a better book the next time. Send a note to me at `babsboyd@me.com`.

Chapter 1

Getting Started with Your iPad

If you ordered your iPad online, if someone gave you an iPad (aren't you lucky!), or if you just prefer to do it yourself, follow the steps in the sections you need to set up. For the most part it's a matter of tapping — but when you have to make a choice, I try to help you make the decision that's right for you (sparing you an overwhelmingly detailed explanation). As soon as your iPad is set up, I show you how to go to the AARP website and explain some basic touchscreen gestures.

tech tip

Most of your decisions will come when you are setting up your Internet connection and your Apple ID. You don't have to connect to the Internet to use your iPad, but an Internet connection does let you use iPad functions to the fullest. So, bear with me. Follow the steps one at a time, and you'll be using your iPad in fewer than 20 minutes (assuming all goes well).

tech 2 to connect

activities

- **Inspecting Your iPad**
- **Setting Up a Wi-Fi Internet Connection**
- **Setting Up a Cellular Internet Connection**
- **Creating an Apple ID**
- **Visiting the AARP Website**
- **Swiping, Pinching, and Zooming**
- **Turning It On and Off**

To complete the setup, you have to tap virtual buttons and scroll a couple times. Tapping means touching the button and then lifting your finger. If you touch and hold the button, nothing happens until you lift your finger. To scroll, place one fingertip on the list and then move your finger forward or backward without lifting it. The list moves up and down. You then lift your finger and tap the item on the list you want to select.

Inspecting Your iPad

If you haven't yet, open the box, lift your iPad out, and unwrap the cellophane protection. Although I recommend using a protective sleeve or cover, the iPad isn't as delicate as it might seem.

Your iPad has a few buttons and holes (called *ports*). You can see their positions in Figure 1-1. Depending on the iPad model you have, the technicalities are slightly different, but they do have the same functions:

- **Home button** takes you to the Home screen. I explain the screen and all its powers in Chapter 2.
- **Front camera** sees you when you are using FaceTime for video chat or Photo Booth, which are explained, respectively, in Chapters 4 and 8.
- **Volume** is changed when you press on the top or bottom of the button. The iPad has to be actively on, known as *awake*, for this button to work.

- **Side switch** can have one of two functions: It can work as a mute button, quieting sounds, or it can be a screen lock button, locking the screen in the portrait (vertical) or landscape (horizontal) view. I tell you about these settings in Chapter 2.

- **On/Off Sleep/Wake** is the button you press and hold to turn your iPad on or off. It's also the button you press quickly once to put your iPad to sleep, which means the iPad is on but not active. Pressing the Wake button or the Home button wakes your iPad. You find more information about this button at the end of this chapter in the section "Turning It On and Off."

- **Back camera** is a camera and video recorder.

- **Microphone** is the tiny hole that picks up your voice or sounds when you are using the dictation feature, recording video, or having a video chat.

- **Headphone jack** is where you plug headphones or speakers.

- **SIM tray** and the SIM ejection hole just above it are on iPads with 3G or 4G capabilities. The SIM ejection tool is in the folded white package with documentation and Apple stickers. I talk about SIM cards a little later in this chapter in "Setting Up Your iPad."

- **Dock connector** is where you plug the Dock Connector to USB Cable to charge the battery. You can see the Dock Connector to USB Cable that came with your iPad in Figure 1-2.

- **Speaker** emits sounds from music, videos, podcasts, alerts, or chats. Adjust the sound with the Volume button on the right side or press the side switch to mute sound completely. Press the side switch again to turn on sound. I show you another way to adjust the volume in Chapter 2.

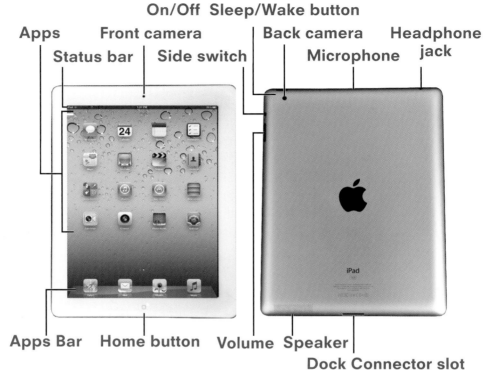

Figure 1-1

Along with your iPad, you get these goodies:

- The Dock connector to USB cable.
- The USB power adapter, which is used to charge the battery on your iPad.
- A little white cardboard envelope, which has legal documents, the SIM Ejector tool (if you have a 3G or 4G iPad), and Apple stickers that can decorate whatever you see fit.

Attach the USB connector...   **Then plug this end into the iPad.**
    to the power adapter.

Figure 1-2

Setting Up a Wi-Fi Internet Connection

All iPads have Wi-Fi, but you must be in a Wi-Fi zone to connect to the Internet. If you have Internet service as part of your television service, you probably have a Wi-Fi zone at home. Wi-Fi uses radio waves to connect to the modem and router that is connected to your Internet service provider (ISP). You need to know your username and password (if you use one) to connect to the Internet on your iPad via Wi-Fi. Many public places such as bars, coffee shops, and airports have free Wi-Fi, and you can access it with your iPad. If those places require a password, you can get it from the person working behind the counter.

These steps show you how to set up your iPad using Wi-Fi you have set up at home.

1. Press and hold the On/Off Sleep/Wake button for two seconds and then let go. The Apple logo, and then the iPad logo appear.
2. Place one finger on the arrow next to the words Slide to Set Up and then slide your finger to the right.
3. Tap the blue-and-white arrow shown in Figure 1-3.
4. Tap your country or region.
5. Tap Next to bring up the Location Services screen.
6. Tap Enable, and then tap the Next button.
7. Tap the network that is yours.
8. Tap the Wi-Fi network password. To access numbers, tap the .?123 key. If you need capital letters, tap the shift key.
9. Tap the Join key (on the keyboard or on the Enter Password window). To change the Wi-Fi network, see the bonus chapter at `http://www.wiley.com/go/ ipadtechtoconnect`.
10. Tap the Next button.
11. Go to the "Creating an Apple ID" section in this chapter and continue from there.

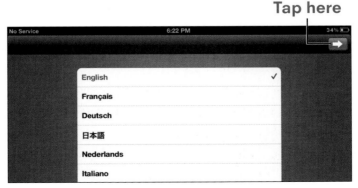

Figure 1-3

Setting Up a Cellular Internet Connection

When you buy a third-generation iPad with 3G or 4G cellular network access, the SIM card is installed and doesn't require a PIN code. You can activate your iPad right out of the box with the preinstalled SIM card. You must, however, have a cellular data account with a cellular provider (such as AT&T, T-Mobile, or Verizon) to use a cellular connection to connect to the Internet or send e-mail.

You can't access the 3G or 4G network until you open a cellular account. When you open the account at a cellular provider store, which may be where you bought your iPad, you get a four-digit PIN (personal identification number) that unlocks the SIM card. You need this PIN to activate the cellular connection.

Make sure you understand the terms of your cellular contract. Using the Internet connection in some areas can lead to unexpectedly high bills, otherwise.

1. Press and hold the On/Off Sleep/Wake button for two seconds and then let go.
2. Place one finger on the arrow next to the words Slide to Set Up and then slide your finger to the right.
3. Tap the blue and white arrow. Refer back to Figure 1-3.
4. Tap your country or region.
5. Tap Next to bring up the Location Services screen.
6. Tap Enable, and then tap the Next button.
7. Tap Use Cellular Connection.
8. Tap in the four-digit PIN code, if requested.
9. Tap OK. You'll see a screen that says Set Up as New iPad.

10. Tap the Next button.
11. If you don't have an Apple ID, continue to the next section. If you do have an Apple ID, tap Sign In. Type your Apple ID and password.

Creating an Apple ID

An Apple ID lets you set up and access iCloud and the App and the iTunes Stores. (You can read more about those topics in Chapters 14 and 10, respectively.) An Apple ID is required if you want to use FaceTime for video chatting and iMessage for text chatting or exchanging messages. It's also necessary to use Find My iPhone to locate your iPad should you lose or misplace it.

Continue from the preceding steps if you don't already have an Apple ID.

1. Tap Create a Free Apple ID.
2. Set your birthday month, day, and year. To scroll, place one fingertip on the month then move your finger forward and backward to scroll through the list. Stop when your birth month is highlighted.
3. Tap Next.
4. Type your first name.
5. Tap Last Name and type it.
6. Tap Next in the upper right corner.
7. If you want to use an existing e-mail address, tap Use Your Current Email Address. If you don't have an e-mail address or want to create one specifically for your Apple ID, tap Get a Free iCloud Email Address and then type in the address you would like to use.
8. Tap Next.

9. If you're using your current email address, type your existing e-mail address in the Email field. If you created an iCloud e-mail, type the name you would like to use. Choose carefully! This will be your Apple ID.

10. Tap Password and type in a password. It should have at least eight characters, including a number, an uppercase letter, and a lowercase letter.

11. Tap Verify and type the password again.

12. Tap Next.

13. Tap Question. Choose a security question from the list.

14. Tap Answer and type in the answer to your question.

15. Tap Next. If someone else already uses that address, you have to choose a different one.

16. If you *don't* want to get e-mails from Apple, tap the button to change it to Off.

17. Tap Next.

18. Tap Agree, and then tap Agree again.

19. After a few minutes, the Set Up iCloud screen appears. Tap Don't Use iCloud.

20. Tap Next.

21. If you want to use Dictation, which means having what you say to your iPad converted to text, tap Use Dictation. You must have an active Internet connection for Dictation to work. Tap Don't Use Dictation if you'd rather not use it.

22. Tap Next.

23. If you want to send diagnostic and usage data to Apple on a daily basis, tap Automatically Send to turn it on. The data includes how you use your iPad and your location.

24. Tap Next.

25. Register your iPad with Apple by tapping Next.

26. Your iPad is now set up. Tap Start Using iPad to open the Home screen, which appears in Figure 1-4.

Figure 1-4

Visiting the AARP Website

Chapter 6 explains the ins and outs of Safari, the web browser app that comes on the iPad, but I want you to do something real right from Chapter 1. What better task than visiting the AARP website?

1. Tap the Safari icon.
2. Tap the Go To This Address field.
3. Type *aarp.* You don't have to type *http://www.*
4. Tap and hold the .com key. Other suffixes appear, as shown in Figure 1-5.
5. Slide your finger to the .org key. Lift your finger when it turns blue.
6. Tap the Go key.
7. The AARP home page opens, looking something like what you see in Figure 1-6.

Other suffixes

Figure 1-5

Tap to sign up

Figure 1-6

To sign up on the AARP website, tap Log In. Tap Register on the page that opens. When you tap the fields on the registration page, you can type in the requested information.

Swiping, Pinching, and Zooming

Don't be alarmed — these aren't the latest slang words for shoplifting. Swiping, pinching, and zooming are, in addition to tap and slide, the touchscreen gestures you need to know. Here's each gesture, just so you have them all in one place:

- **Tapping:** Like tapping someone on the shoulder, a tap is a quick touch without any holding and it's probably the gesture you use most frequently. Tap an app's icon to open the app. Tap an item in a list to select it. Tap the letters on the keyboard to type. Variations on tapping follow:

  - **Tap and hold:** Use the tap-and-hold trick on keys that have accented variants, such as the vowels, the N, S, C, and Z. Some of the punctuation keys offer variants too: the dash, the period, question mark, and exclamation point.

  - **Double-tap:** Zoom in and zoom out of a web page, e-mail message, or photo with a quick tap-tap. A double-tap also changes the shift key on the keyboard to caps lock. (You have to enable that function in Settings. Tap General, and then tap Keyboard). A single tap zooms in on a map, but to zoom out on a map, you need the next trick.

  - **Two-finger tap:** In the Maps app, a two-finger tap zooms out of a map; tap twice with a single finger to zoom in again and again and again right up to the street level.

- **Scrolling:** Scrolling is a dragging motion. Scroll with one, two, or three fingers — but not four or five. Touch the screen with your fingertip(s) and drag your finger up or down. In some apps and websites, you can scroll left or right too. Scrolling is most often used to go through a list. Scrolling doesn't select or open anything; it only moves the list. You must tap to select.

- **Swiping:** Sometimes swiping is referred to as *flicking*. Touch the screen with one, two, or three fingers and quickly swipe up, or left, or right, and away (as if you were brushing a crumb off the table). Swiping left and right on the Home screen moves to the next or previous screen; I explain that in Chapter 2. Swiping in a list, instead of scrolling, moves the list up and down more quickly. You can wait for it to stop or tap to stop the moving list. Then tap the option you want.

  Swiping *up* with four fingers reveals the open apps bar. Swiping *down* with four fingers closes it. Swiping left to right with four fingers switches between open apps. You can read about the open apps bar and having more than one app open at a time in Chapter 2.

- **Pinching:** Pinch a finger and your thumb together to zoom out; pinch out, in the opposite direction to zoom in. You can do this for photos, websites, and apps such as Mail or things you read in Newsstand. Figure 1-7 shows a pinch.

  Pinch all fingers and your thumb together to return to the Home screen from any app.

- **Sliding:** Slider bars show up when you want to turn your iPad on or off, or unlock it, as shown in Figure 1-8. Touch and hold the arrow on the slider bar, sliding left or right. Whatever action is listed on the slider bar is what happens.

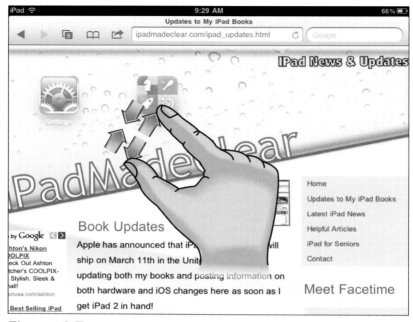

Figure 1-7

Slider bar

Figure 1-8

Turning It On and Off

Your iPad has different states of consciousness. You can control them with the On/Off Sleep/Wake button on the top right of your iPad.

- **On** means your iPad responds when you press either the home button or the On/Off Sleep/Wake button. To turn on your iPad, press and hold the On/Off Sleep/Wake button for a few seconds and then release it. When Slide to Unlock appears at the bottom of the screen, drag your finger from left to right across the slider. If you have a 3G or 4G iPad, tap Unlock to enter the PIN code or tap OK to use your iPad without the cellular data network. (In that case, you can still use Wi-Fi.)
- **Wake** is when you see something on the screen or hear something coming out of the speaker. Press the On/Off Sleep/Wake button or the home button to wake your iPad.
- **Unlocked** means your iPad is awake and the touchscreen is active. After turning on or waking your iPad, drag the slider bar to unlock. Refer back to Figure 1-8. Your iPad can be locked and awake, which means you can listen to music and adjust the volume, but nothing happens when you touch the touchscreen. See Chapter 12 to read about playing music on your iPad.
- **Sleep** is when the touchscreen is dark but the iPad is on. Nothing happens when you touch the touchscreen and you aren't listening to music. Press the On/Off Sleep/Wake button to lock and put your iPad to sleep. Your iPad automatically locks itself and goes to sleep if you don't touch the screen for 2 minutes. You can change this setting to up to 15 minutes or to Never. I explain how to change the setting in Chapter 15. Putting your iPad to sleep saves battery power and keeps you from unintentionally opening an app by accidentally touching the home screen.

■ **Off** means your iPad doesn't respond when you press the home button. To turn off your iPad, press and hold the On/Off Sleep/Wake button for a couple of seconds, and then release. Drag the Slide to Power Off bar. Tap the Cancel button if you change your mind.

If you use an iPad Smart Cover from Apple with an iPad 2 or third-generation iPad, you can set your iPad to automatically unlock and lock when you open and close the cover. Read how in Chapter 14.

Chapter 2

Finding Your Way Around

Y ou'll do some things, such as pressing the home button and managing apps, every time you use your iPad. Others are once-in-a-while tasks such as adjusting volume or brightness, locking screen orientation, and searching. The last section takes you through the status bar icons, which tell you the time and give you information about your iPad's Internet connection, battery charge, and incoming messages.

tech tip

Activating accessibility features (see "Opting for Accessibility" later in this chapter) can make your iPad experience easier, especially if you have limited sight or dexterity.

tech to connect

activities

- **Going Home (Screen)**
- **Adjusting the Volume**
- **Changing the Brightness and Wallpaper**
- **Locking the Screen Orientation**
- **Using Spotlight to Search**
- **Starting, Switching Between, and Closing Apps**
- **Organizing Apps and Folders**
- **Opting for Accessibility**
- **Reading Notifications, Alerts, and Badges**

Going Home (Screen)

When you turn on or unlock your iPad, what you see is the Home screen. Home is where you can open apps and get to the Spotlight search screen (the app that finds things on your iPad and beyond).

The round, slightly depressed button centered beneath the screen on the iPad frame is the home button, and it's pointed out in Figure 2-1. Press it to go places:

- Press the home button once when your iPad is sleeping to wake it up (the same way as the On/Off Sleep/Wake button does).

- Press the home button once to return to the Home screen at any time in any app or on any other Home screen. (If you have more than 26 apps, you can flick to get to other Home screens.)

- Press the home button once when you're on the first Home screen to open Spotlight Search.

- Quickly press the home button twice when your iPad is awake (when you're on a Home screen or in Spotlight Search or an app) to open the open apps bar (also known as multitasking bar). The bar shows open apps, and looks similar to what you see in Figure 2-1. Tap any of the apps in the bar to go to that app.

- If your iPad is locked or sleeping, quickly press the home button twice to show three sets of commands, as shown in Figure 2-2:
  - Playback commands (to pause, play, fast-forward, or rewind music)
  - Volume slider
  - Picture Frame mode button, which displays the photos stored on your iPad in an ongoing sequence

Volume slider
Playback commands

Home button

Figure 2-1

Picture Frame mode button

Figure 2-2

Adjusting the Volume

You may need to adjust the volume while you're listening
to music, watching videos, or making FaceTime calls. And,
you can separately set the volume for notifications and alerts
(which let you know you have an incoming e-mail, iMessage,
FaceTime request, or reminder). You can choose a different
sound effect for each alert, and you can assign a specific
sound effect to individual contacts. (Chapter 5 is all about
contacts.) The volume is the same, however, for all sound
effects.

Refer back to Figure 2-1 to see where the volume button is.
Push the top part of the button to raise the volume; push the

bottom part to lower the volume. Figure 2-3 shows me adjusting the volume while I'm watching a YouTube video.

Here's how to choose the sound for an alert:

1. Tap the Settings icon on the iPad Home screen.
2. Tap General.
3. Tap Sounds. The options appear, as shown in Figure 2-4.
4. Drag the volume slider to put the sound where you want it.
5. Tap Ringtone.
6. Tap the sound you want. It plays when you tap it.
7. Tap the Sounds button, which looks like a fat left-facing arrow.
8. Repeat steps 5 through 7 to change the sound effects for other alerts. You can choose None for any alert except Ringtone.

Appears when you adjust volume

Figure 2-3

Figure 2-4

Changing the Brightness and Wallpaper

Sometimes, depending on where you use your iPad and your eyesight, you may need to adjust the brightness of the screen. Follow these steps:

1. Tap the Settings icon on the Home screen.
2. Tap General.
3. Tap Brightness & Wallpaper.
4. Drag the Brightness slider to adjust.

Wallpaper is the background image you see on the lock and Home screens. You can use the same image on both or a distinct image for each. Here's how:

1. Tap the Settings icon on the Home screen.
2. Tap General.
3. Tap Brightness & Wallpaper.
4. Tap the space where you see the images of iPad lock and Home screens, as pointed out in Figure 2-5.
5. Tap Wallpaper (or one of the other choices such as Camera Roll, Photo Stream, or an album from the Photos library if you want to use a photograph that you've taken with your iPad).
6. Tap an image from the selection that appears to see a preview.
7. Tap one of the following:
   - *Cancel* lets you see other choices.
   - *Set Lock Screen* uses the image as your lock screen.
   - *Set Home Screen* uses the image as the background for your Home screen.
   - *Set Both* sets the image as your wallpaper for both the lock and home screens.

You can quickly adjust the brightness and volume when your iPad is awake: Double-click the home button on the open apps bar and swipe from left to right. The brightness and volume sliders appear, as shown in Figure 2-6.

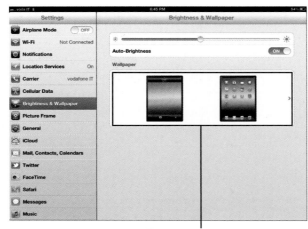

Tap this space

Figure 2-5

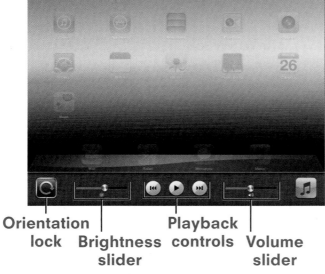

Orientation lock   Brightness slider   Playback controls   Volume slider

Figure 2-6

Locking the Screen Orientation

If you rotate your iPad 90 degrees, the screen rotates too. In that case, you're switching between a portrait and landscape view. Some things — movies, videos, or games — are better viewed in landscape. You may prefer looking at web pages or your calendar in landscape. Sometimes typing is easier in landscape view because the keyboard is bigger. It's all a matter of personal preference. But some apps only work in one view.

You can lock the orientation — so it won't switch when it's rotated — in either portrait or landscape view:

1. Double-click the home button.
2. Swipe to the right.
3. Tap the orientation lock button, which is pointed out in Figure 2-6. The icon appears in the status bar to remind you that it's on.
4. Tap the button again to unlock the orientation.

You can set the side switch so it works as an orientation lock button. Tap Settings, tap General, and then tap Lock Rotation under Use Side Switch To. A checkmark means that function is selected. When selected, a Mute button appears on the open apps bar when you swipe right.

Using Spotlight to Search

Spotlight is the feature to use for finding things stored on your iPad or on the web. When you start using Spotlight from the Home screen, your search — defined by a word, phrase, or number — encompasses all the apps that are on your iPad: e-mail, notes, contacts, reminders, calendars, and so on. Spotlight searches your iPad for any items that match your search criteria. For example, if I type in the name John, I get results showing contacts named John, songs by Johnny Cash, e-mails exchanged with anyone named John, appointments with John, and any Dear John notes I've written.

You can use Spotlight within many apps; any time you see the magnifying glass icon, you can tap it to open Spotlight and follow the preceding steps. When you search from within an app, however, Spotlight searches only within that app and sometimes only for certain information. In Mail, for example, only sender, recipient, and subject line are searched, and in Contacts, first, last, and company names.

Follow these steps to perform a Spotlight search:

1. Press the home button.
2. Type your word or phrase in the blank field at the top of the screen.
3. Tap Search.
4. Tap an item in the list to view that item's contents, or scroll down and tap Search Web and Search Wikipedia.
5. Tap the item you want to see.

Starting, Switching Between, and Closing Apps

To launch — that's computer speak for open — an app on the Home screen, tap the app icon. That's it: Tap and go. After you do what you want to do in the app, press the home button to return to the Home screen. When you leave an app by pressing the home button, the app is still on in the background. This means you can have multiple apps open at the same time, although you only see one app at a time on the screen.

Apple insists you don't need to quit apps you aren't using, but some apps — like radio show apps — keep using some of iPad's memory and power, even when they're in suspended animation. Call me compulsive, but I regularly double-click the home button and close apps I'm not using.

To switch between one app and another, do the following:

1. Double-click the home button.
2. Swipe left or right to move through the open apps.
3. Tap the app you want. If you change your mind, tap the screen to return to the active app.

To completely quit an app removes it from the open apps bar (but not from your iPad). To quit an app, follow these steps:

1. Double-click the home button.
2. Press and hold any of the app buttons.
3. Tap the minus sign on the app you want to close.
4. Press the home button.

Organizing Apps and Folders

You can rearrange apps so that the ones you use most frequently are at the top of the home screen. Also, you can group apps together in a folder. For example, you could put all gaming apps in a Games folder. You can move apps in and out of the apps bar (aka dock), too. I am moving the Maps app in Figure 2-7.

These steps explain how to rearrange apps:

1. Press and hold any app button on your Home screen.
2. Drag the apps where you want them. To go from one Home screen to another, drag toward where you want it.
3. When you like the arrangement, press the home button.

Putting like-minded apps together in a folder helps you find them easily. Each folder can hold up to 20 apps and you can put folders, instead of apps, on the dock if you want.

1. Press and hold any app on the home screen.
2. Lift your finger after the apps start wiggling.
3. Drag one app icon over another app icon. The folder opens beneath the icon, as you can see in Figure 2-8.
4. iPad assigns a name. To change the folder name, go to the next step. To keep the assigned name, skip to step 8.
5. Tap the name in the field.
6. Tap the X at the right end of the field.
7. Type the name you want for the folder.
8. To add another app to the folder, tap the folder.
9. Drag the app into the folder.
10. Tap the home button.

Figure 2-7

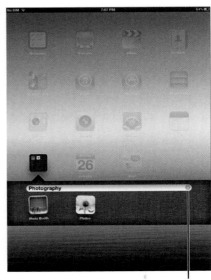

Tap here to delete the name

Figure 2-8

tech tip

To move apps out of folders, follow these steps:

1. Press and hold any app on the Home screen.
2. Lift your finger after the apps start wiggling.
3. Tap the folder that holds the app you want to remove.
4. Drag out the app. A folder is automatically deleted when it's empty.

Opting for Accessibility

The iPad is chock full of features that let you customize the screen, making it more accessible for users with varying levels of physical challenges. The features are divided into three categories: Vision, Hearing, and Physical & Motor. I briefly explain each feature, but I recommend consulting Chapter 24 of the iPad User Guide for complete instructions. Consider asking someone to help you set up the options from which you would most benefit. To get the chapter, go to manuals.info.apple.com/en_US/ipad_user_guide.pdf.

To access these options, follow these steps;

1. On the Home screen, tap Settings.
2. Tap General.
3. Scroll down and tap Accessibility. The screen you see in Figure 2-9 opens.
4. Tap the item you want to customize (or turn off).

Figure 2-9

The following functions fall into the Vision category:

- *VoiceOver:* Play an audible description of the onscreen buttons. Within VoiceOver, you can adjust the following:
    - *Speak Hints* — VoiceOver can offer hints about what to do.
    - *Speaking Rate* — Touch and drag the slider to adjust how fast the VoiceOver instructions are spoken.
    - *Typing Feedback* — Reads what you type as you type it. Choose from characters, words, or both.
    - *Use Phonetics* — VoiceOver reads a letter and then gives a phonetic equivalent, such as *s* and then *sam*.
    - *Use Pitch Change* — Use a higher or lower voice to indicate when letters are added or deleted, or when a list of items is started or finished.
    - *Use Compact Voice* — Improve the quality of the VoiceOver voice.
    - *Braille* — Attach a Braille device.
    - *Rotor* — Choose when you want to use a rotor, which is a control that changes gestures.

- *Language Rotor* — Assign a language to the rotors.
- *Navigate Images* — Choose how you want VoiceOver to navigate images.
- *Speak Notifications* — VoiceOver can speak the notifications that arrive.

- *Zoom:* Enlarge the entire iPad screen when you double-tap with three fingers. Use three fingers to move the screen around. Double-tap again with three fingers to return to normal size. You can't use VoiceOver and Zoom simultaneously.

- *Large Text:* Choose a text size, from 20 point to 56 point, for Calendar, Contacts, Mail, Messages, and Notes.

- *White on Black:* All color is inverted, like a photo negative, which is particularly useful when reading text.

- *Speak Selection:* This function reads selected text out loud, even if VoiceOver is turned off.

- *Speak Auto-text:* While you're typing, any corrections iPad automatically makes are spoken out loud.

One function helps users who have a hearing impairment: The Mono Audio function changes the left and right sound channels into a single channel that comes through both sides so those who can hear with only one ear hear both parts.

These two functions are in the Physical & Motor section:

- **AssistiveTouch:** You can use an accessory, such as a joystick, to control your iPad, and you can create custom gestures to replace the standard multitouch gestures.

- **Triple-Click Home:** Associate triple-clicking to the home button with one of the Accessibility functions: VoiceOver, Zoom, AssistiveTouch, or White on Black.

Reading Notifications, Alerts, and Badges

You get notifications when a new message arrives from Mail, Messages, or FaceTime, and when you have scheduled a reminder about a deadline, task, or event on Calendar or Reminders. (Read more about scheduling reminder notifications in Chapters 9 and 13.)

- An alert can be a sound, a message, or both. You choose the type of alert you want for different apps. For example, you can hear a sound when a new e-mail arrives and see a brief message on the iPad screen too.
- Badges are red circles that have either a number or exclamation point inside. (See Figure 2-10.) The number is how many unread messages you have or apps you need to update. An exclamation point means there's a problem that needs your attention (for instance, you tried to send a message but it didn't go through).

Open the Notification Center, shown in Figure 2-10, by swiping downward from the status bar. Read the notifications and tap them one at a time if you want to respond, for example, to an incoming e-mail. The FaceTime app's Notification Center settings are shown in Figure 2-11.

You choose if and how you want to be notified by doing the following:

1. Tap Settings.
2. Tap Notifications.
3. Tap an option:
   - *Manually* means you put the apps in the Notification Center in the order you want to see them.
   - *By Time* means that notifications are listed in the order they arrive.

4. In the list on the right, tap the app whose notifications you want to customize.

5. Tap On for Notification Center. Notifications that are on always appear in the Notification center, regardless of whether you choose to receive an alert (Step 6).

6. Under Alert Style, tap one of the following:

   ▪ *None.* You won't get an alert. The notification, however, will be in the notification center when you drag from the status bar.

   ▪ *Banners.* They appear at the top of the screen and then go away.

   ▪ *Alerts.* They appear in the center of your iPad, and you have to respond before they will disappear.

7. Tap On for Badge App Icon to see a badge that shows the number of unanswered requests or messages you have.

8. Tap On for View in Lock Screen to let your iPad receive notifications even when it's locked and sleeping.

9. Tap the Notifications button at the top of the screen.

10. In the list on the right, tap the next app whose notifications you want to customize.

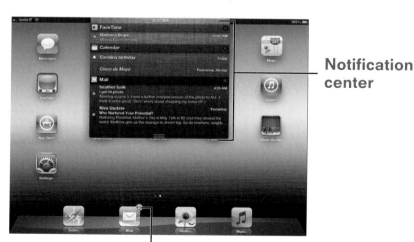

Notification center

This badge indicates 2 unread messages

Figure 2-10

Figure 2-11

In Mail and Messages, tap On for Show Preview to see the first two lines of incoming mail and messages. In Messages, you can repeat an alert up to 10 times.

Chapter 3

Using the Keyboard and Communicating via E-mail

E-mail is a great way to stay in touch with the kids, grand-kids, current and former friends and coworkers, your book club and community groups — you name it. And with your portable iPad, it's easier than ever. In this chapter, I show you how to set up your e-mail account using your Apple ID. (If you haven't done so, return to Chapter 1 and create one.) I then explain addressing, writing, and sending e-mail.

tech to connect

activities

- **Setting Up Your E-mail Account**
- **Typing and Sending an E-mail Message**
- **Finding Hidden Keys on the Keyboard**
- **Editing Text**
- **Receiving and Reading Messages**
- **Replying to, Filing, and Deleting Messages**
- **Working with Multiple Messages**
- **E-mailing from Other Apps**
- **Setting Font Size and Adding a Signature**

And with all the comings and goings of e-mail messages, you'll want to know about filing and deleting messages and finding and re-reading favorite missives from your loved ones. At the end of the chapter, I show you how to send e-mail from other iPad apps, such as Notes and Maps. And since you'll be typing a lot, I review the ins and outs of using the iPad's keyboard.

Setting Up Your E-mail Account

The folks where you bought your iPad are more than happy to help you set up your e-mail account, but if you happen to be an independent type or you change your e-mail service provider (which means changing the setup on your iPad), this section can help. Setting up (known also as *configuring*) your e-mail account takes a few minutes and a series of taps.

If you already have the following e-mail services, you need to have just your e-mail address and password handy because the technical information is already on your iPad:

- AOL
- Google Gmail
- iCloud
- Microsoft Exchange
- Microsoft Hotmail
- Yahoo!

The following steps help you set up the Mail app no matter which of these e-mail service providers you use. The only difference is that some ask you to enter your name and an account description in addition to your e-mail address and password. Follow these steps to set up e-mail on your iPad:

1. Tap Mail on the Home screen.
2. Tap the service you use. (For example, I tap iCloud because that's what I use.)
3. Type in your e-mail address and password. It's your Apple ID for iCloud.
4. Tap Next.
5. Tap an option and tap On for it. You'll see a screen like the one in Figure 3-1.
6. Tap Save.

Figure 3-1

Sunshine on a cloudy day

iCloud is a way to store information somewhere else (on the proverbial cloud). I use iCloud because I use Apple products, but there are other cloud storage options. When I enter information on my iPad (such as a name and address in Contacts), the data goes to my iCloud account. That way, if I lose the information somehow, I can get it back from iCloud (versus trying to remember and retype everything). If you have other electronic devices, like a computer or an iPhone, and you use iCloud on those devices, the information in each category you turn on via your iPad will be synchronized with those devices. That means the same information in all of those places.

Typing and Sending an E-mail Message

After your e-mail account is set up, you can send a message to someone. You need two things:

- The e-mail address of the person you want to send the message to, and the e-mail address must be exact: One small difference and the message either won't be delivered or will be sent to the wrong person.
- A Wi-Fi or cellular Internet connection to send your e-mail message.

If you want to try this but don't know any e-mail addresses yet, send me a message, telling me how you like the book. Type in *babsboyd@me.com*. Follow these steps:

1. Tap the Mail icon on the Home screen.
2. Tap the new message icon in the upper-right corner; the icon is pointed out in Figure 3-2 and looks like a piece of paper and pencil.
3. Tap in the To field.

4. Type the e-mail address of the person to whom you're sending the message. If you want to send the same message to more than one person, type a comma after each e-mail address.

5. Tap the Return key.

6. Type the subject.

7. Tap Return.

8. Type the message you want to send. The keyboard is slightly bigger in landscape (horizontal) view, which can make typing easier.

9. Tap the Send button in the upper-right corner of the message.

New message icon

No Message Selected

Figure 3-2

Adjust the keyboard settings by tapping Settings, then General, then Keyboard. Tap On for the options you want to enable. If you want to add other languages or those fun smiley faces known as emoticons (see Figure 3-3), follow these steps:

1. Tap International Keyboards in the Keyboard settings.

2. Tap Add New Keyboard.

3. Scroll to and tap the language you want to add. To switch between keyboards of different languages, tap the globe button.

Finding Hidden Keys on the Keyboard

Use these tactics to find keys you don't see on the keyboard:

- Tap the .!123 key in the lower-left corner to find the missing semi-colon along with its friends the slash, parentheses, and numbers zero to nine. The keyboard changes to that shown in Figure 3-4.

- Tap #+= on the right to reveal more symbols, as shown in Figure 3-4.

- Tap the ABC or 123 key to return to the previous keyboard layouts.

- Hold the ABC key and slide your finger to the symbol or number you wish to type. The character is typed but the keyboard reverts to letters.

- Tap the keyboard key in the lower-right to hide the keyboard; tap the message (or wherever you were typing) to reveal it again.

- Tap Delete (the key known to Windows users as Backspace) in the upper right to erase one letter at a time. Tap and hold the key to speed up.

- Touch and hold keys for letters, such as the vowels, that have accents. Then drag your finger to the accented letter you want and lift.

- Tap the shift key to capitalize a letter. Double-tap the shift key to type in all caps.

- Double-tap the space bar to insert a space and a period at the end of a sentence.

Figure 3-3

Shift key

Tap to hide keyboard
Tap to reveal more symbols

Figure 3-4

Take this down

When my thumbs get tired, I turn on Dictation to let iPad do the typing for me. You must have a third-generation iPad and an active Internet connection for it to work. To dictate messages, do the following:

1. Tap the Mail app.

2. Tap the New Message button.

3. Tap the microphone key on the keyboard.

4. Speak your message and say punctuation marks.

5. Tap Done. Tap the microphone key again to make corrections.

Editing Text

You can select text and make it bold, italicized, or underlined; you can indent sentences or paragraphs. You can cut, copy, and paste selected text somewhere else in the message or in a different message or even in a different app, such as Notes or Reminders.

If iPad thinks you are misspelling a word, it makes a suggestion just below the word you're typing. As you type, iPad adjusts the suggestions or deletes it entirely. Tapping the spacebar means you accept the correction. Sometimes iPad is comically, or dreadfully, wrong. Look carefully at what you typed before sending a message. You can turn off auto-correction in the keyboard settings.

Tap once to insert the cursor somewhere in the middle of your text, then follow these steps:

1. Double-tap a word to highlight it and activate grabbers, as shown in Figure 3-5.
2. Touch and drag the grabbers to highlight the words you want to edit, and then lift your finger.
3. Tap the button that corresponds to what you want:
   - Cut eliminates the text completely but stores it temporarily in a virtual clipboard so you can paste it somewhere else in the message or in a different app, such as Notes.
   - Copy leaves the text where it is but also stores a copy of the text in the temporary clipboard so you can paste it somewhere else.
   - Paste appears when you have either cut or copied something and is the command you tap to insert the cut or copied text.
   - Suggest appears if you select just one word; you get a list of synonyms.

4. Tap the arrow to the right to see these options:

- BIU opens a button bar with bold, italic, and underline options, which you tap to format the selected text.
- Define shows a definition of the word (but only if you've highlighted one word).
- Quote Level offers increase (indent) or decrease (outdent) options.

To undo your edit, carefully shake your iPad. Tap the Undo button on the message that appears. Just (gently) shake your iPad again to redo what you undid.

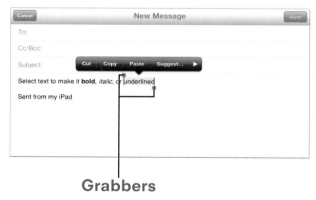

Grabbers

Figure 3-5

Receiving and Reading Messages

When an e-mail message arrives in Mail, you *can* get several alerts on your iPad depending on how you set up your notifications. Change your alerts by following these steps:

1. From the Home screen, tap Settings.
2. Tap Notifications.
3. Tap Mail.
4. Tap each option and choose On or Off:
   - *Notification Center:* On to see incoming messages in the Notification Center.
   - *Alert Styles:* None to receive no alert; Banner to see a fleeting notice across the top of your iPad screen; or Alert to see a message that you must acknowledge.
   - *Badge App Icon:* On for the home screen's Mail icon to show a badge with the number of unread messages.

To read your messages, do the following:

1. Tap Mail on the Home screen. The number next to Inbox shows how many unread messages you have. Figure 3-6 shows there are 5.
2. In portrait view, swipe from left to right to open the Mailboxes drawer; tap outside the drawer to close it. (In landscape view, the screen is split in two sections, as shown in Figure 3-7.)
3. Tap Inbox.
4. Tap the message you want to read. Unread messages have a blue dot.
5. Tap Mark (or Details) to do one of the following:
   - Flag the message, which puts a flag next to it in the message list.
   - Mark the message as unread, which returns the blue dot next to the message in the list.
6. To read another message, tap it in the Inbox list.

The number of unread messages

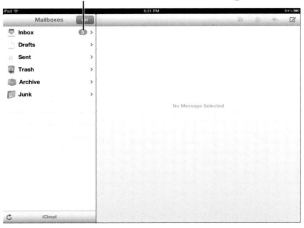

Figure 3-6

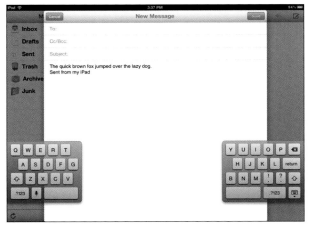

Figure 3-7

Replying to, Filing, and Deleting Messages

When you get an e-mail, chances are you want to respond somehow. You can file, delete, reply, forward, or print a message. The respective icons are pointed out in Figure 3-8.

To do any of these actions, take the following steps:

1. Tap Mail on the Home screen.
2. Tap Inbox.
3. Tap the message.
4. To file or delete the message, go to step 5. Otherwise, skip to step 6.
5. Tap one of the buttons:

   - Tap the File button (which looks like a file folder). Then tap the folder where you want to put the message. If you tap File by mistake, just tap the blue Cancel button.

   - Tap the trashcan button to delete your message. You can change the setting to be asked before a message is deleted. Those steps follow.

6. Tap the Reply/Forward/Print button, which looks like an arrow. Three choices appear, as shown in Figure 3-8:

   - Tap Reply to send an e-mail back to the sender of the message. If more than one person got the original message, tap either Reply (reply only to the sender) or Reply All (reply to *all* the recipients; careful there!). Type the message and tap Send.

   - Tap Forward to send the message to someone else. If a file was attached to the original message, tap to also send the attachment (or not). Tap in the To field and type the e-mail address of the person who should get the forwarded message. Then tap Return. Tap the upper part of the message body if you want to type your own message in addition to the forwarded message.

- Tap Print to print the message. You must have an AirPrint-compatible printer on your Wi-Fi network to do this. If you do, tap Print, tap Printer to select the networked printer, and then tap Print again.

Tap to delete message
Tap to open mailbox

Tap link to go to website

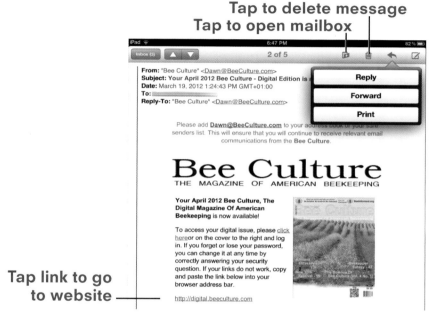

Figure 3-8

I've been known to accidentally delete a message. I changed that possibility when I followed these steps. Now, I get asked before a message is deleted.

1. Tap Settings.
2. Tap Mail, Contacts, Calendars.
3. Tap On for Ask Before Deleting.

Working with Multiple Messages

Sometimes you want to do the same thing to many messages. Instead of doing something one message at a time, you can select multiple messages and then

- Delete them.
- Move them to another folder.
- Mark them as unread.
- Flag them.

Here's the way to do these things:

1. Tap the Mail app on the Home screen.
2. Tap the folder (Inbox, Trash, or the like) that has the messages you want to work with.
3. Tap the Edit button.
4. Tap the circle next to the messages you want to delete (or move or flag).
5. Tap the button you want, as shown in Figure 3-9:
   - Delete
   - Move
   - Mark

You can swipe the message in the list to bring up a red Delete button. Tap the Delete button. Remember that if you delete part of a string of messages (replies back and forth from a single conversation), you delete the entire exchange.

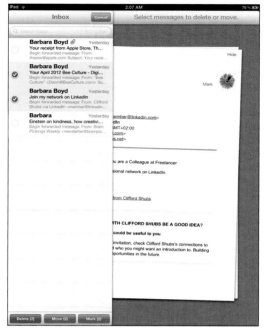

Figure 3-9

E-mailing from Other Apps

You can send your lists, photos, and web page URLs by e-mail to someone directly from within the app. (You can do the same with map locations but the process is a little more complicated so I left that explanation for Chapter 7.)

The steps for sending notes, photos, and web pages are the same. The only difference is from which app you start:

1. Tap Notes (or Photos or Safari) from the Home screen.
2. Go to the note, photo, or web page you want to e-mail.

3. Tap the Action button (a rectangle with an arrow; it's pointed out in Figure 3-10). In Notes the icon is at the bottom of the screen; in Photos and Safari it's at the top.

4. Tap Email (Mail Link to This Page in Safari).

5. Address the message as explained at the beginning of this chapter.

6. *Optional:* Tap in the Subject field and message body field and type what you prefer.

7. Tap Send.

Action button

Figure 3-10

Setting Font Size and Adding a Signature

Mail has two settings that I find especially helpful: font size and signature. Regarding the font setting: Incoming messages appear as the minimum font size. That way, you don't have to fiddle around if someone sends you a message written in a miniscule type. The name, address, and subject lines remain the standard size. A signature is the line that appears at the end of every e-mail message you send. The default is *Sent from my iPad.*

To adjust these two recommended settings, follow the steps:

1. Tap Settings on the home screen.
2. Tap Mail, Contacts, Calendars.
3. Tap Minimum Font Size. Your screen will look like Figure 3-11.
4. Tap the size you want.
5. Tap the Mail, Contacts button at the top of the Minimum Font Size screen.
6. Tap Signature.
7. Delete *Sent from my iPad.* Type what you want to appear in the signature line. Your name and contact information are standards. Some people add a credited quote.
8. Press the home button (on the iPad frame) to leave the Settings app.

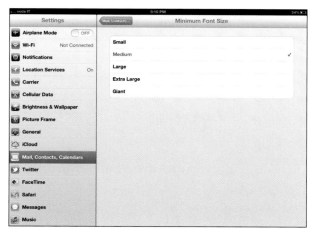

Figure 3-11

Chapter 4

Chatting with FaceTime and Messages

Your iPad comes with two great apps that can help you stay in touch with friends, family, and colleagues who use Apple products. (That includes Bernie, Betty, and Uncle Bob, and an iPad, iPhone, iPod Touch, or Macintosh computer.) You can exchange written messages instantly and make video calls.

tech 2 to connect

activities

- **Setting Up FaceTime**
- **Making a FaceTime Video Call**
- **Adding to FaceTime Favorites**
- **Answering a FaceTime Call**
- **Writing and Sending Messages**
- **Adding a Photo to a Message**
- **Receiving and Replying to Messages**
- **Deleting and Forwarding Messages**

In this chapter, I show you how to set up FaceTime using your Apple ID. If you prefer to type versus talk and see the other person, Messages will be one of your favorite apps. Messages sends instant communication from your iPad to other Apple products like the iPod touch and iPhone. I explain how to address, write, and send messages, and then show you how to read incoming messages and respond. With all these incoming and outgoing messages, you'll want to clean up. I give you the steps for doing that, too.

If you haven't created your Apple ID, please go to Chapter 1 and follow the steps that explain how to do so. You'll need it to use FaceTime and Messages.

Setting Up FaceTime

Before you can use FaceTime, you have to set up your FaceTime account and ID. The app uses e-mail addresses to make and receive calls, which means your FaceTime ID will be the e-mail address you set up in Chapter 3.

Follow these steps to set up FaceTime:

1. Tap Settings on the Home screen.
2. Tap FaceTime in the Settings column. The FaceTime Settings screen opens, looking like Figure 4-1.
3. Tap in the Name field.
4. Type your Apple ID. If you haven't made one, go to Chapter 1. It explains how.
5. Tap in the Password field.
6. Type your password.
7. Tap the Sign In button.
8. If the Email field shows an e-mail address, tap the Next button. If your Apple ID *isn't* in the form of an e-mail

address, go to step 9. The Email field is your FaceTime ID. Other people use that e-mail to call you on FaceTime.

9. Type your e-mail address.

10. Tap Next. The e-mail address is verified and the FaceTime screen appears, like you see in Figure 4-2.

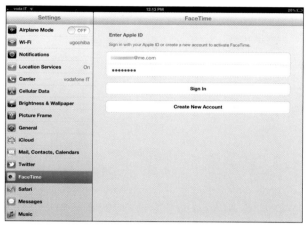

Figure 4-1

Figure 4-2

Making a FaceTime Video Call

You need these things to make a FaceTime call:

- An iPad 2 or third-generation iPad
- A Wi-Fi connection. (See Chapter 1 if you're unsure about this.)
- The FaceTime ID of the person you want to call.
- An activated FaceTime account. (The task previous to this one tells you how to do that.)

The person you want to FaceTime call needs to have two things:

- An iPad 2 or third-generation iPad, an iPhone 4/4S or later, a fourth-generation iPod touch, or a Macintosh computer with the FaceTime app.
- A FaceTime ID.

tech tip

Before you start, the person you're calling must have her device on and unlocked and be connected to Wi-Fi. In other words, you have to use the telephone to call or send an e-mail message to set up a time to FaceTime (or just try a FaceTime call). If the person you're calling isn't available, you'll get a message to that effect.

To start a FaceTime call, follow these steps:

1. Tap FaceTime on the Home screen.
2. Tap the Contacts button.
3. If the person's FaceTime ID is in Contacts, skip to step 10. If not, tap the Add (+) button to create a record in Contacts. See Chapter 5 to read more about using the Contacts app.
4. Tap in the First field; type the person's first name. See Figure 4-3.

5. Tap in the Last field; type the person's last name.

6. Tap in the Home field; type the person's e-mail address (or, if calling the iPhone, that number). Type the address *exactly*.

7. Tap Ringtone. A ringtone is the sound you hear when someone calls you.

8. Tap a ringtone. A checkmark indicates the ringtone you chose.

9. Tap Done. The contact is added to your Contacts.

10. Tap the person you want to call. If you've made that person a favorite, tap Favorites and tap the person's name. A blue video camera icon appears next to the e-mail address or iPhone number that is FaceTime-enabled.

11. Tap the e-mail address on the Info screen. A FaceTime call starts. When the person accepts your call, you see her face on your iPad. Your face is in a smaller window. You can see my face in the smaller window in Figure 4-4.

12. Talk for as long as you like and do any of the following during your call:

   ▪ Rotate your iPad to change orientation.

   ▪ Tap the Switch Camera button to switch between front and back cameras. One tap shows your surroundings (such as your snoring spouse or a beautiful sunset). Tap it again so the person you're speaking with sees you.

   ▪ Tap the Mute button so the person can't hear you. You can still hear her and you can both see each other. Tap the Mute button again to let her hear you.

   ▪ Drag your image to where you want it.

   ▪ Use another app. Tap the Home button and open another app. You can still hear each other, but you can't see each other.

13. Tap End when you want to hang up.

Figure 4-3

Mute Who called
Who I called
Tap to show your surroundings

Figure 4-4

Adding to FaceTime Favorites

Figure 4-5 shows the tabs at the bottom right of the FaceTime screen. Tap a tab to open one of the following options:

- *Favorites* are contacts that you designate as favorites. It's helpful to mark the people you call frequently. You take care of the Favorites list when you're using FaceTime.
- *Recents* shows outgoing FaceTime calls and any incoming FaceTime calls (missed or answered).
- *Contacts* lets you view the Contacts app in FaceTime. You can also make FaceTime calls from the Contacts app, which I explain the Chapter 5.

Figure 4-5

If you call someone often, put that person in the FaceTime Favorites list by doing the following:

1. Tap FaceTime on the Home screen.

2. Tap the Contacts tab at the bottom of the FaceTime screen.

3. Tap the person's name in the Contacts list.

4. Tap Add to Favorites.

5. Tap the Favorites tab at the bottom of the FaceTime screen.

6. Tap the name to start a FaceTime call.

Answering a FaceTime Call

When your iPad is on, unlocked, and connected to Wi-Fi, you can receive and answer FaceTime calls. If your iPad is off, sleeping, locked, or not connected to Wi-Fi, the caller will receive a message that you are unavailable and the next time you unlock your iPad, a badge appears on the FaceTime button on the Home screen with a number that indicates how many FaceTime calls you missed. You also see these calls in the Recents list.

To respond to an incoming call, do the following:

1. You hear a ringtone. FaceTime automatically opens, like you see in Figure 4-6. But instead of my face there, you'll see yours.

2. Tap Accept to answer the call. Tap Decline if you don't feel like talking.

3. Conduct your conversation the same way as if you had initiated the call.

4. Tap End when your conversation is finished.

Figure 4-6

Writing and Sending Messages

Your iPad has an instant messaging app — aptly named Messages — that is similar to text messaging with your cell phone. You type and send a message. If the person you sent it to is available right then, he can respond immediately. An onscreen icon (it looks like ellipses) lets you know if he's writing; then his message appears. You write your response, and then send it and so on.

You can even send messages to groups of people. You can exchange instant messages (aka IMs) with other folks who have an Apple product, including an iPad, iPhone, or iPod touch that is using the operation system (OS) 5.0.

To send an IM, follow these steps:

1. Tap Messages on the Home screen.
2. Tap the New Message button, which looks like a piece of paper with a pencil on it. The first time you open Messages, you might see the message shown in Figure 4-7.
3. If you don't see the iMessage window, skip to step 7. If you do see the iMessage window, go to step 4.
4. Tap in the Password field; type your Apple ID password.
5. Tap the Sign In button. Another iMessage window confirms the e-mail address that will receive messages.
6. Tap Next. Your e-mail address is verified and the New Message window opens, as shown in Figure 4-8.

New Message button   **Add button**

Figure 4-7

Figure 4-8

7. Tap the Add (+) button to open Contacts. Tap the name of the person you want to send a message to, and then tap his e-mail address or phone number. Or, type the e-mail address or phone number of the person you want to message.

Only an iOS 5 device, such as an iPhone, iPad, iPod touch, or a Mac with the Messages app, can get this kind of message.

8. Tap the Add (plus symbol) button if you want to send the message to more than one person and repeat step 7.

9. Tap in the Text field.

10. Type your message.

11. Tap Send. Your message appears in a blue bubble on the right and in the Messages list on the left, as shown in Figure 4-9.

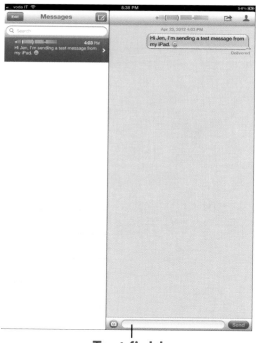

**Text field
(Tap here and type your message)**

Figure 4-9

Adding a Photo to a Message

You can add a photo to a message:

1. Tap Messages on the Home screen.
2. Tap the New Message button.
3. Tap the Camera button that's pointed out in Figure 4-10.
4. Tap an option:
   - *Take Photo or Video.* Tap the Camera button to take a photo. Tap the Use button or tap Retake to try again, and then tap Use.
   - *Choose Existing.* Tap the album that has the photo. Tap the photo. Tap Use.
5. Add more pictures by restarting at step 3.
6. Type your message.
7. Tap Send.

Camera button

Figure 4-10

Receiving and Replying to Messages

Messages are arranged in conversations, which means that the entire exchange of messages with another person (or group) is stored as one collection, called a *conversation*. The messages are enclosed in conversation bubbles. This organization lets you view the exchange on one screen rather than opening and closing a series of messages. Your incoming and outgoing messages appear in chronological order in the Messages list.

When you get a message, you'll see a badge on the Messages button. If banner alerts are turned on, you see a notification there too. Both a badge and banner appear in Figure 4-11.

To read the message, follow these steps:

1. Tap the Messages button on the Home screen.
2. Tap the message you received. The messages that you've written are in blue bubbles toward the right. The messages that you've gotten are in gray bubbles toward the left.
3. Tap in the text field.
4. Type your response. You can see me typing a reply in Figure 4-12.

5. Tap the Send button.

6. If the person responds immediately, you will see an ellipsis in a gray bubble. When he taps Send, you see the message.

tech tip

If you are instant messaging, it's courteous to let the other person know when you're finished by typing *Got to run* or *See you later, alligator.*

Badge shows number of new messages
Banner alert indicates messages

Figure 4-11

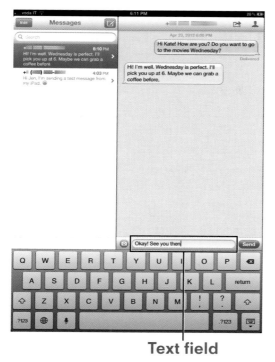

Text field

Figure 4-12

Deleting and Forwarding Messages

The Messages screen can get congested. You have the choice to delete an entire message conversation or delete single messages.

To delete an entire conversation, follow these steps:

1. Tap the Messages button on the Home screen.
2. Tap the Edit button at the top left of the screen. A white minus sign in a red circle appears next to each conversation.

3. Tap the minus sign next to the conversation you want to delete. A Delete button appears and the minus sign tips, as shown in Figure 4-13.

4. Tap the Delete button. Or, tap the minus sign again if you change your mind.

5. Tap Done when you finish deleting conversations.

Selected messages are removed from a conversation, but a conversation remains regardless — even if you delete all the messages in it. This makes it easy to send a new message to this person without searching in your Contacts or Favorites lists. Just tap the conversation, type your message, and tap Send.

To delete a message within a conversation, follow these steps:

1. Tap the Messages button on the Home screen.

2. Tap the conversation. All the messages are in blue and gray bubbles on the right.

3. Tap the Action button (an arrow shooting out of a rectangle) in the upper right. Circles appear next to each message; two buttons (Delete and Forward) appear at the bottom.

4. Tap the circle next to the message you want to delete. A white checkmark in a red circle appears next to the selected messages; see Figure 4-14.

5. Tap the Delete button. Or, tap the Clear All button to delete all the messages in the conversation at once.

To forward a message or messages within a conversation to someone else, follow these steps. Keep in mind that you don't want to breach privacy.

1. Tap the Messages button on the Home screen.

2. Tap the conversation. All the messages are in blue and gray bubbles on the right.

3. Tap the Action button (arrow and rectangle).

4. Tap the circle next to the message(s) you want to forward. A white checkmark in a red circle appears next to the selected messages.

5. Tap the Forward button. A new message is created, and it has all the selected messages together in the text field.

6. Tap the Add (+) button to choose a recipient from Contacts or type the phone number or e-mail of the person to whom you want to forward the messages.

7. Tap the Send button.

8. Tap the Home button to return to the Home screen.

Tap to delete a conversation
This button has been tapped

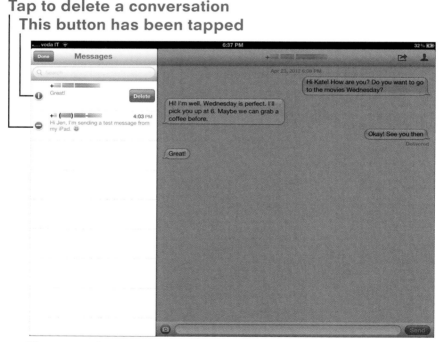

Figure 4-13

Messages chosen for deletion
Tap here to avoid having to choose

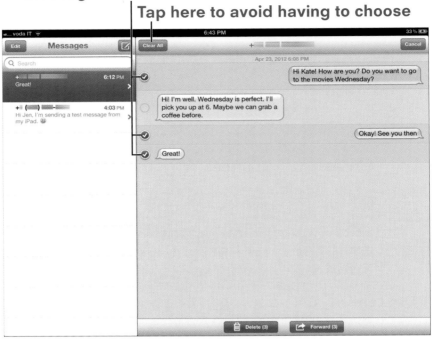

Figure 4-14

Chapter 5

Tracking Addresses with Contacts

This chapter introduces what I think is one of iPad's most useful capabilities — creating an electronic address book. With people moving around so much these days, you're going to update often. Contacts is the electronic address book app on your iPad. The tasks in this section take you through the steps to create new contacts, and then later editing or deleting contacts. I show you how to view and sort your contacts and how to search for a person or company. At the end of the chapter, I go through the ways Contacts interacts with other apps.

tech 2 to connect

activities

- **Creating New Contacts**
- **Adding Fields**
- **Adding a Photo to a Contact**
- **Viewing and Sorting Contacts**
- **Editing and Deleting Contacts**
- **Searching Contacts**
- **Interacting with Other Apps**

Creating New Contacts

With new contacts, you can add not just name, address, and phone number but a person's photo, birthday, or anniversary — which links to Calendar — e-mail address, and website. And if that isn't enough, you can create any other kind of field you want to invent (like account number or shoe size).

You don't *have* to have first and last names for a contact; you can use a company name instead. In fact, you can leave blank any other field that you don't have information for. If you just have the name and phone number of a person or company, you can fill in only those fields. Contacts automatically capitalizes the first letter of fields that are usually filled in with proper nouns, such as First Name, Last Name, and City.

Follow these steps to create a new contact and fill in as much information as you want about that contact:

1. Tap Contacts on the Home screen.
2. Tap the plus sign at the bottom of the page. A new contact screen opens, as shown in Figure 5-1.
3. Type in a name for your contact.
4. Tap Return to move to the next field; do that each time you type in a field.
5. Tap in and type information for these fields, as well, if you like:

   ▪ *Mobile:* A cellphone number goes here. Contacts automatically formats phone numbers with dashes or parentheses.

   ▪ *Home:* A home phone number goes here.

   ▪ *Home Page:* The keyboard changes to include the @ symbol and a .com key when you type in this field. Hold and slide the .com key for other suffixes, such as .net, .org, and .edu.

■ *Notes:* The field can hold any information you want. For example, you could jot down gift ideas for that person or the hours a store is open.

6. *Optional:* Tap Ringtone to assign a special sound to the contact. When that contact sends a message or requests a FaceTime call, you know by the sound who is getting in touch.

7. Tap Add New Address to enter a street address. The screen will expand to look like Figure 5-2.

8. Optional: To change the field name, tap the field name itself. Tap the label you want to associate with the field or tap Add Custom Label and then type.

Tap to open a new screen

Figure 5-1

Figure 5-2

Adding Fields

The Contacts Info form contains what iPad considers the most commonly used fields. You can add these fields with the following steps:

1. Tap the Add Field button to open the list shown in Figure 5-3.
2. Tap the field you want to add:

   ■ *Prefix:* Add a field before First Name, so you can type in a title such as Dr. or Prince.

   ■ *Related People:* Add people, such as parent, spouse, or sibling (or, for a company, an assistant or manager). After tapping the option, you return to the Info screen. Tap the field label to reveal a list of choices for the type of relation, tap the relation, and then type in the relation's name.

   ■ *Phonetic First Name:* You can type in a pronunciation.

   ■ *Phonetic Last Name:* Go ahead; type in that pronunciation.

   ■ *Middle:* It goes between the first and last name.

   ■ *Suffix:* To add common suffixes like M.D. or Jr.

   ■ *Nickname:* Goes before Company.

   ■ *Job Title:* Goes before Company

   ■ *Department:* Goes before Company.

   ■ *Twitter:* Add a Twitter user name.

   ■ *Profile:* Add a user name for Facebook, Flickr, LinkedIn, or MySpace, or a custom service. After tapping the Profile option, the Info screen re-opens. As soon as you begin typing a user name in the field, a new Profile field appears beneath it. Tap the field label to the left of user name to choose which social network you want.

■ *Instant Message:* After tapping this option, you return to the Info screen. Type the user name; tap the field below; tap the correct service or add a custom service.

■ *Birthday:* Set the person's birth date. Any birthday you add here appears in Calendar if you activate the birthday calendar. Read more about Calendar in Chapter 9.

■ *Date:* You can add more than one memorable date.

3. Repeat steps 1 and 2 for as many fields as you want to add. After you use an option, it no longer appears in the Add Field options list.

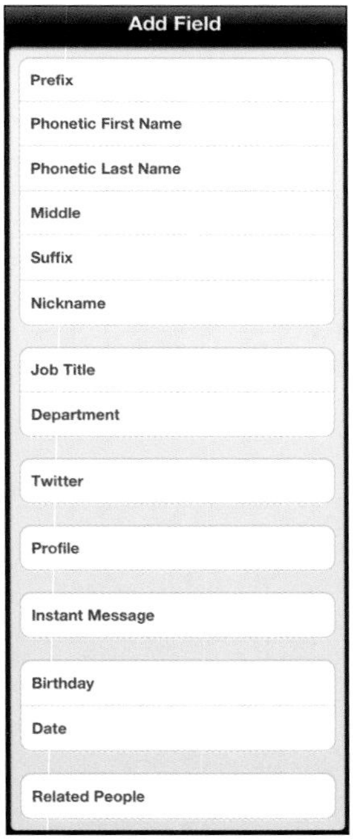

Add Field
Prefix
Phonetic First Name
Phonetic Last Name
Middle
Suffix
Nickname
Job Title
Department
Twitter
Profile
Instant Message
Birthday
Date
Related People

Figure 5-3

Adding a Photo to a Contact

You can add a photo of the contact. When that contact makes a FaceTime call, his or her picture appears on your screen. You can add a photo two ways.

This method requires that the person actually be with you:

1. Tap Add Photo.
2. Tap Take Photo.
3. Aim the iPad at your subject. (Tap the Switch Camera button in the upper right if you see yourself instead of your subject. The button's pointed out in Figure 5-4.)
4. When you like what you see, tap the green camera button.
5. *Optional:* Tap Retake, if you want to try again.
6. Pinch and spread to zoom in on the subject's face and drag to move it to the center of the screen. It will be much smaller on the Contact Info screen.
7. When you like the result, tap Use Photo. You see the photo you took in the photo field on the Contact Info screen.

Your contact doesn't have to be with you for this method to work, but you'll need to have the photo in your Camera Roll:

1. Tap Choose Photo.
2. Tap Camera Roll or the album where the photo you want to use is stored.
3. Tap the photo you want to use.
4. Re-size it by pinching or spreading your fingers on the image and drag it to the position you want.
5. When you like the photo, tap Use Photo. The photo is saved to the New Contact screen. Figure 5-5 shows how a completed contact might look.

Switch Camera button

Tap to take picture

Figure 5-4

Tap the index to search for someone

Figure 5-5

Viewing and Sorting Contacts

In Contacts, you can adjust the sort order and the display order. Each can be sorted by either first or last name and you can combine the options in four different ways. I prefer to sort by last name and display by first name, but you should choose whatever makes the most sense to you. Follow these steps to make your selection:

1. Tap Settings on the Home screen.
2. Tap Mail, Contacts, Calendars.
3. Scroll down to the Contacts section shown in Figure 5-6.
4. Tap Sort Order.
5. Tap the sort order you want to use:
   - *First, Last* sorts by first name (so you'd find a person named Bob Zink under B). If you have more than one Bob in Contacts, all the Bobs are sorted alphabetically by last name.
   - *Last, First* sorts by last name (so you'd find Bob Zink under Z).
6. Tap Display Order.
7. Tap the option you want to use:
   - *First, Last* displays the contact name as Bob Zink.
   - *Last, First* displays the contact name as Zink Bob.
8. Tap the display order you want to use.
9. Press the Home button on the iPad frame.

Create a new contact for yourself and include your relatives. After you've done that, tap My Info in Settings; then tap Mail, Contacts, Calendars. Contacts opens and you can choose the contact you created for yourself. The information will be accessed by Safari when you fill out forms online.

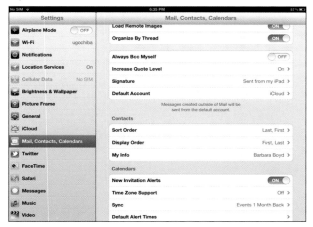

Figure 5-6

Editing and Deleting Contacts

Now when Uncle Bob moves to Florida, or when you two have a major falling out and you refuse to talk to him, you can make the change in Contacts. The process for editing and deleting contacts starts the same:

1. Tap Contacts on the Home screen.
2. Tap the name of the contact you want to edit.
3. Tap the Edit button at the bottom of the page.
4. Tap in the fields you want to edit.
5. To delete a field from this contact, do one of the following:
   - Tap the red and white minus sign to the left of the field, and then tap the Delete button that appears, as shown in Figure 5-7.
   - Tap the field you want to delete and then tap the X that appears to the right.

You can delete a contact entirely, instead of deleting just a field:

1. Tap Contacts on the Home screen.
2. Tap the name of the contact you want to delete.
3. Tap the Edit button at the bottom of the page.
4. Scroll down to and tap Delete Contact, which is shown in Figure 5-7.
5. Tap Delete when you're asked to confirm the action.

Figure 5-7

Searching Contacts

If you have fewer than 13 contacts, you can see them all at once on the screen; feel free to skip this section. If you have more, you'll need to know how to search for a person or company.

There are different ways to search contacts that I've outlined here:

1. Tap Contacts on the Home screen.
2. In the index that runs down the right side of the screen, tap the letter that corresponds to the name. Names are sorted and displayed (as set up in the viewing and sorting section). Refer back to Figure 5-5; it shows the index.
3. Scroll through that section of the alphabet to find the person. Tap it when you find it.

Here's another way to look:

1. Tap Contacts on the Home screen.
2. Tap in the Search field.
3. Type the person's name. A list of possible matches appears. As you type more, the choices are fewer. See Figure 5-8.
4. Tap the name.

I've typed only this

This is what has appeared

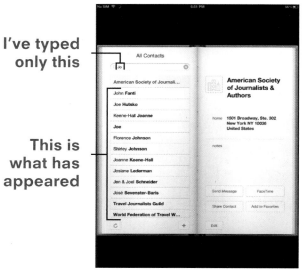

Figure 5-8

Interacting with Other Apps

Other apps on your iPad use the information you enter in Contacts. For example, Mail and Messages tap in to Contacts to help you address the messages you want to send. FaceTime shows Contacts on its main screen so you can find names and numbers of people you want to call. Contacts also appears when you want to send things from non-communication apps like Photos, Maps, and Safari.

You can access some apps from Contacts itself by doing the following:

1. Tap Contacts on the Home screen.
2. Tap the contact you want to work with. (The previous section in this chapter gives searching tips.)
3. Tap a field on the Contact Info screen. Depending on what you tap, you'll see the following:
   - *E-mail Address* opens a new message in Mail, addressed to the contact. Type a subject and a message and tap Send.
   - *Phone Number* tries to initiate a FaceTime call if the contact uses the phone number for his FaceTime identity. (Read all about FaceTime in Chapter 4.)
   - *URL* opens the web page in Safari.
   - *Address* opens Maps to the location. See Figure 5-9.
4. Or, tap one of the buttons at the bottom of the info screen. They are shown back in Figure 5-8:
   - *Send Message* opens a message, addressed to this contact, in Messages.
   - *FaceTime* tries to initiate a FaceTime call with this contact.
   - *Share Contact* lets you send this contact information to another person. It is sent via Mail or Messages.
   - *Add to Favorites* puts this contact in the Favorites category on FaceTime; read more about this in Chapter 4.

Any time you see a To field, tap the + (plus symbol) on the right side of the field to open a Contacts search screen, as explained in the previous section "Searching Contacts."

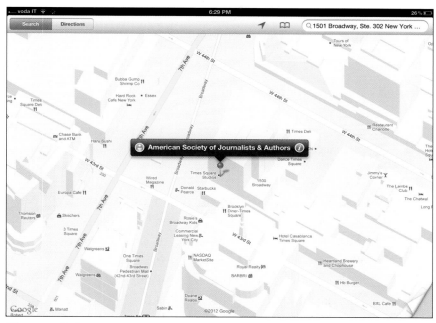

Figure 5-9

Chapter 6

Surfing the Web with Safari

In Chapter 1 you use Safari, iPad's web browser app, to go to the AARP web page. That just whets your whistle. This chapter shows you more about Safari. The World Wide Web, mostly referred to as just *the web,* or *online,* is a vast collection of information on just about everything. Having a great collection but not being able to find anything is just plain frustrating, so this chapter kicks off by explaining how to use your iPad to find online what you're looking for. I take you through a few different ways you can visit specific websites and how to work with the different parts of a web page.

tech to connect

activities

- Searching the Web
- Visiting Websites
- Opening Links
- Retracing Your Steps with History
- Marking and Organizing Bookmarks
- Sharing and Saving Web Pages

The remaining tasks in this chapter focus on the features and functions both Safari and iPad offer for maneuvering around the web. Three tasks are related to web pages themselves: going back to a web page you viewed previously, bookmarking web pages you want to revisit in the future, and sharing web pages with others.

Searching the Web

Looking for something specific on the web sometimes feels like searching for a needle in a haystack. Two things can keep you on track and I explain them here:

- Using reliable, respected search engines, such as Bing, Google, or Yahoo!
- Carefully defining your search terms.

Your iPad has Google set as the pre-loaded search engine. You can change that. Tap Settings, tap Safari, tap Search Engine, and then tap a search engine of your choice. Whichever you choose is what automatically opens when you go to Safari. For the search tasks in this chapter and elsewhere in this book, I use Google.

To search the web using Safari's search feature, do the following:

1. Tap the Safari app on the Home screen.
2. Tap in the search field (where you see the word Google).

3. Type whatever you're searching for. Say you're planning a vacation to Paris and want to find a hotel. If you type *paris,* you get a list of suggested matches like those you see in Figure 6-1. If you're more specific by typing *paris france hotels,* your results look like what you see in Figure 6-2.

4. Do one of the following:

   ■ Tap a suggested match.

   ■ Tap the Search key and ignore the suggested matches.

5. Tap the link that most closely matches what you're after. The results with a yellow background are matches based on your search criteria, but are also part of Google's paid advertising. They catch your eye, but the better match may be further down the list.

Tap here in the search field

Figure 6-1

Previous button

URL field

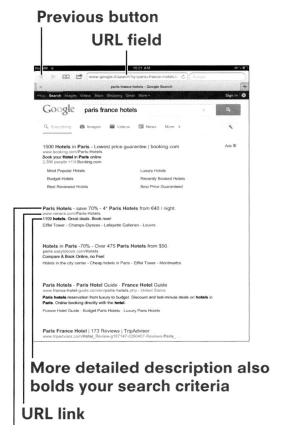

More detailed description also bolds your search criteria

URL link

Web page description bolds your search criteria

Figure 6-2

6. Scroll down to the bottom of the page and tap TripAdvisor.

7. Tap No Thanks when you're presented with a free TripAdvisor app (you can always install it later); see Figure 6-3.

8. Tap the Previous button at the top of the screen. The button is pointed out in Figure 6-2.

9. Tap one of the other results to see if it's closer to what you're looking for.

10. When you find a website that seems to meet your needs, tap it. For even more help, go on to "Opening Links" in this chapter for help wading through what you see onscreen.

It's small

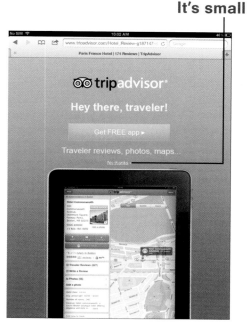

Figure 6-3

Lots of companies offer iPad-specific apps. Using an iPad-specific app makes that website easier to navigate, so it makes sense to download the apps for websites that you visit often. Chapter 10 has more to say on this topic.

The amount of information on a web page can be overwhelming, but you can search within a web page, much like you search the web itself. Type the word or phrase you hope to find on the page. A list of suggested matches on the web appears first, but at the top of the keyboard is a Find On Page option. Tap that to search within the web page.

Visiting Websites

Companies and organizations tend to put their website address (their URL) in their print advertising or announce them on TV and radio. When you visit your banker, baker, or insurance broker, chances are both e-mail and website addresses are printed on the business card. A lot of publications offer content you can only get online. You have plenty of opportunities to use Safari with a particular address.

Just follow these steps if going to a specific URL:

1. Tap Safari on the Home screen.
2. Tap the URL field — where it reads Go To This Address.
3. Type the address of the website you want to visit. (For example, I typed *aarp.org*. You don't have to type *http://www.*) As you type, websites you've visited appear, as in Figure 6-4. You can stop typing and tap one if it's where you're headed. If not, go to the next step.
4. Finish typing the URL and tap the Go key.

Would you like to start another search but keep the one you started? Tap the new tab button to open another web page on another screen. The new tab button is pointed out in Figure 6-5. The web page you were viewing moves back and a new blank web page with blank URL and search fields opens. You can have up to nine web pages open at once.

5. Tap the X to the left of the page name (on the tab) to close the web page.

Instead of searching for a company, try typing the company name in the URL field, and follow it with *.com*. See if its website opens. And remember, in Safari there's a convenient .com key on the keyboard; hold it and slide for other suffixes, such as .net, .org, and .edu.

Previously visited websites

URL field

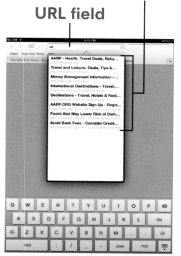

Figure 6-4

Press and hold link to see these options

New tab button

Figure 6-5

Opening Links

A website is a collection of web pages. When you type the URL for a company or organization, that address launches the first, or opening, page of the website. Links are on that first page. When you tap a link, you perform an action or go to another web page within the site. (For example, clicking a Register link on a company's first page takes you to another page where you can sign up as a member.)

1. Press and hold a link. You'll see options like those in Figure 6-5.

2. Tap the option you want:
   - *Open* opens the web page.
   - *Open in New Tab* forces Safari to open the web page link in a new Safari page screen (instead of replacing the web page you're looking at).
   - *Add to Reading List* puts the link in your reading list so you can come back later. Read more about the reading list in "Marking and Organizing Bookmarks."
   - *Save Image* is visible only if the link is an image. Saves the image to the Photos app.
   - *Copy* copies the URL to the clipboard so you can paste it elsewhere, like in an e-mail message or a note. (That way someone else can click the URL and go to the page.)

3. If the link opens another app, *double-click* the home button (on the iPad frame), and tap Safari to return to the web page you were viewing.

When you're on a web page, tapping a link can bring up other options, too:

- Open a new message in Mail to communicate with the company.
- Show a graphic, photo, or photo slideshow you can tap through.
- Open a map that shows the address you tapped on the web page.
- Play an audio file, such as a news story, podcast, or song.

- Play a video file. It'll probably be better watched in landscape mode. Keep in mind that it takes about 10 seconds for the audio or video file to begin playing. The playback controls appear on the screen and disappear a few seconds after playback begins. Tap the screen to make them appear again.
- Display a form with fields you can fill in with information. When you tap in a field, the keyboard opens. Tap the Next and Previous buttons at the top of the keyboard to move between fields. Figure 6-6 shows a form that I have filled out. Safari accesses your information from Contacts if you created a contact for yourself. Refer to Chapter 5.
- Display a document. Safari can display many popular document file types, including Microsoft Word, Excel, PowerPoint documents, and PDF documents.

Other on-screen controls you may encounter are pop-up menus, often indicated by a downward-pointing arrow, like the one shown in Figure 6-7. Tap it to display the pop-up menu, and then tap your choice. This type of control, as well as check boxes and radio buttons, is common on shopping or survey sites, where you have to make choices. Just tap your way through to mark the boxes and circle on and off.

Figure 6-6

Tap to open pop-up menu

Radio buttons

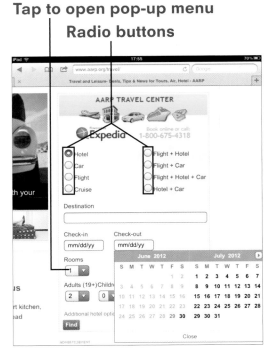

Figure 6-7

Reader all about it

Sometimes I run across something that I wasn't expecting to find but is interesting. If I tap a link that leads to an article, a Reader button can appear in the URL field. This means you can view the article in Reader, which displays the text on a plain white page, without any distracting images, ads, or headlines, as shown in Figure 6-8.

Tap the font button in the upper left to change the size of the text. Tap the action button to reveal options such as printing the article or saving the link to your reading list. Tap either the Previous or Reader button to return to the original web page.

Tap to change text size

Tap either to go to original web page

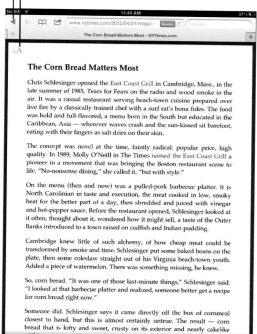

Figure 6-8

Retracing Your Steps with History

When you begin tapping links on a web page and moving from one page to another, you may wind up not knowing how to go back from whence you came. Luckily, Safari records all your movements and you can go back, and then forward again, by tapping the Previous and Next buttons at the top left of the page. The Previous button takes you back one page at a time, but you can retrace your steps across the web right up to where you begin. The Next button repeats your steps forward to the furthest web page you visited before you backtracked *away* from that furthest point by tapping the previous button.

In a nutshell:

- Tap the Previous button to go back to the web page you viewed.
- Tap the Next button to go forward to a page you were viewing before you tapped the Previous button.

Another way to view your Safari web history is via the History folder. Here are the steps:

1. Tap the Bookmark button, which looks like an open book at the top of the screen. It's pointed out in Figure 6-9.
2. Tap the History folder.
3. Tap the Earlier Today folder to see what pages you visited earlier in the day. Tap a previous day's folder to see pages you visited before today.
4. Tap any listed web page to revisit that page. Tap the open web page to return to it.

Bookmark button

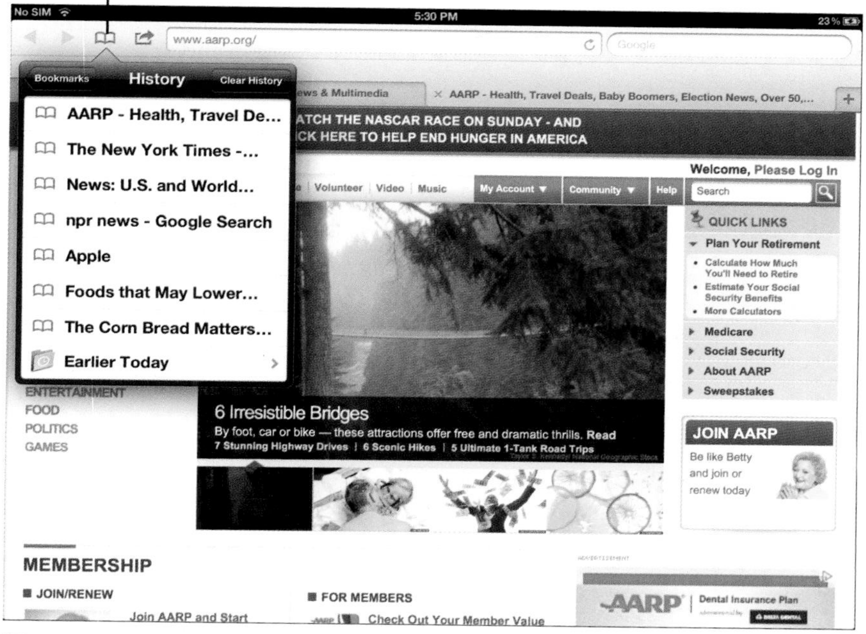

Figure 6-9

You also can clear your history with these steps, which somewhat protects your privacy. That way, no one who borrows your iPad can see where you've been online.

1. Tap the Clear History button (at the top right of the History list). The Clear History button appears at the bottom of the list, giving you a moment to decide whether you really want to erase your web history.

2. Tap Clear History if you want to go through with it; tap Cancel if you don't.

Marking and Organizing Bookmarks

Going through your viewing history is one way to return to a web page you like. Creating a bookmark for your favorite website is more efficient if you expect to go back to that page in the future. After you bookmark a web page, tapping the bookmark takes you directly to that web page.

To create a new bookmark for a web page you're currently viewing, do the following:

1. Tap the Action button, which is pointed out in Figure 6-10.
2. Tap Add Bookmark. The Add Bookmark window opens.
3. Tap the X to the right to delete the automatic name.
4. Type an intuitive name for the bookmark.
5. *Optional:* Tap Bookmarks at the bottom of the window and then tap one of the following:
   - *Bookmarks Bar* to store the bookmark in the space that runs across the top of the Safari screen, just under the URL and search fields. Bookmarks there appear like buttons. Just tap to open the web page.
   - *Bookmarks "Folder"* to store the bookmark under the Bookmarks folder (News, Business, Travel, and the like) you select.
6. Tap Save.

Bookmark menu   Tap to delete name
Action button   Bookmarks bar

Backspace key

Figure 6-10

tech tip

1. Tap the home button on the iPad frame.
2. Tap Settings.
3. Tap Safari.
4. Tap On for Always Show Bookmarks Bar.

You can create subfolders within the Bookmarks folder; that way you can divide your bookmarks by category. For example, you could make a Travel folder and within that folder bookmark several sites, such as AAA, `www.aarp.org/travel`, Carnival Cruise, or Frommer's.

To create a bookmark folder, follow these steps:

1. Tap the Bookmark button at the top of the page.
2. Tap Edit at the top right.
3. Tap New Folder in the upper left.
4. Type a name for the folder.
5. Tap the Bookmarks button in the upper left. Your folder will show a folder icon, which is pointed out in Figure 6-11.
6. Tap Done.
7. Tap outside the Bookmarks window to return to the web page.

You can put folders of bookmarks in the bookmarks bar, and then tap the folder to display the bookmarks within.

1. Tap the Bookmark button.
2. Tap Edit.
3. Tap the folder you want to put on the bookmarks bar.
4. Tap Bookmarks (the field under the folder name).
5. Tap bookmarks bar.
6. Tap elsewhere on the screen to close Bookmarks.

To rearrange your bookmarks, follow these steps:

1. Tap and hold the Rearrange button next to the bookmark you want to move. The Rearrange button, which looks like three stacked lines, is pointed out in Figure 6-11.
2. Drag the button and bookmark where you want it.
3. Release your finger to drop the bookmark in its new location.

To delete a bookmark or bookmark folder, follow these steps:

1. Tap the Remove button. It's the red and white – (minus symbol) to the left of a bookmark or folder.
2. Tap the Delete button. The bookmark or folder disappears.

Folder icons

Bookmark button

Rearrange buttons

Tap to delete bookmark or folder

Figure 6-11

Sharing and Saving Web Pages

Safari offers several ways to save and share web pages. Bookmarking is one way, as explained in this chapter's "Marking and Organizing bookmarks."

Follow these steps to try another way:

1. Tap the Action button at the top of the Safari screen. Figure 6-12 shows the options that come up.

2. Tap one of the following choices:

- *Add to Reading List* places a link to the specific article on the web page in your reading list so you can access it later. (Whereas a bookmark links to the web page itself where the content may change.) Take a look at this chapter's sidebar, titled "Reader all about it," to know more about the reading list.

- *Add to Home Screen* creates an icon, called a web clip, on your Home screen. Tapping it takes you to the website. You can see a web clip icon pointed out in Figure 6-13.

- *Mail Link to This Page* opens, in Mail, a new message that has a link to the web page. Address the message, type your message, and tap Send. The message is sent and you wind up at the web page in Safari.

- *Tweet* attaches a link to the page to a tweet in Twitter. You need to have a Twitter account to perform this action.

- *Print* opens the Printer Options window, which lets you choose a printer and the number of copies. A printer must be connected to the same Wi-Fi network your iPad is connected to.

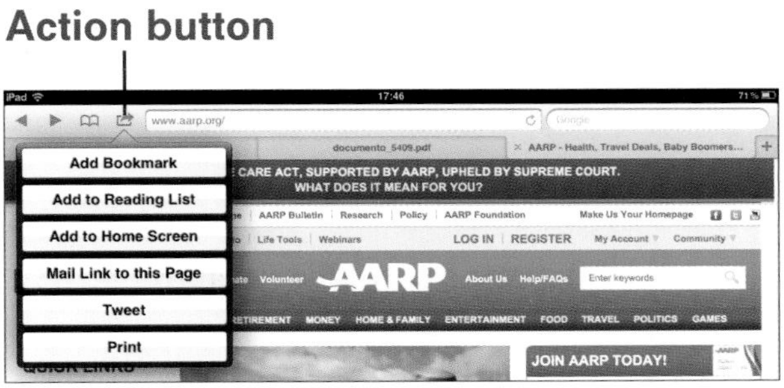

Action button

Figure 6-12

Tapping this web clip icon takes me to the website
Figure 6-13

Spreading the joy

I've seen some pretty amazing things on the web, and sometimes I feel compelled to share the joy (or shock). When I want to share or save an image that I see on a web page, I follow these directions:

1. Press and hold on the image.

2. Tap Save Image to save that image file to the Photos app. Or, to copy it, go to step 3.

3. Tap Copy.

4. Tap the home button on the iPad's frame.

5. Tap another app's icon, such as Mail, Messages, or Notes.

6. Create a new message or note.

7. Double-tap.

8. Tap Paste. A link to the image appears.

It is important to note, however, that saving images to file or copying images could violate copyright law. If you want to share an image you see on a web page, you may want to just share the link to the web page. Otherwise, you could need permission to copy the image.

Chapter 7

Making Travel Plans with Maps

Many people — me included — are fascinated with maps. This chapter's first task shows you how to find your current location and how to see it on different types of maps. I then explain how to look for a specific address or place. Yes, a place. Based on where you are, or where you intend to be, Maps offers suggestions for restaurants, bookstores, pharmacies, mechanics — whatever you might need at a given moment. From Maps, you can access addresses for people or companies that you have in Contacts and search for those addresses. The next task shows ways to use the addresses that you run across in Maps. That way, you can save an address for future reference or share an address with someone else. Last but not least, I explain how to use Maps to find driving directions from one address to another, be it on foot, by car, or by public transportation. In all, you may find Maps is one of the apps you tap into again and again.

tech to connect

activities

- **Viewing Your Current Location with Maps**
- **Searching for an Address or Service**
- **Finding an Address in Contacts**
- **Saving and Sharing an Address**
- **Asking for Directions**
- **Watching Traffic**

Some hints for viewing a map in Maps:

- Double-tap with one finger to zoom in. Repeat as needed.
- Double-tap with two fingers to zoom out. Repeat as needed.
- Pinch in or out with one finger and your thumb to zoom out and in, respectively. (See Chapter 1 for what this looks like.)

Viewing Your Current Location with Maps

I can think of a few reasons you might want to find your present location on a map:

- You need a starting point to know how to get there from here. (Maybe you're driving across town to a place you've never been before or walking somewhere while on vacation.)
- You want to send your location to someone else so they know how to get here from there.
- You're lost.
- You want to see the really cool ways Maps has of viewing your location.

Follow these steps to get around Maps and see where you are from a different viewpoint:

1. Tap the Maps app on the Home screen.
2. Tap the Tracking button (it looks like an arrow) at the top of the screen.
3. If a dialog says "Maps Would Like to Use Your Current Location," tap Okay. A blue dot indicates your precise location.

4. Tap the Tracking button again to line up the map with the direction you're facing. A flashlight beam emanates from the blue dot and a compass appears in the upper right to indicate the direction you're facing.

The circle around the blue dot indicates how precise your location is: The smaller the circle, the more exact the indication. If the circle is pulsing, the location is approximate. When you move, either by walking or driving, the blue dot moves too.

5. Tap the blue dot. You will see the exact address and two buttons, like you can see in Figure 7-1.

6. Tap the Street View button, which is a person in an orange dot. You see the street just as if you are walking on it. Figure 7-2 shows an example of street view. Try the following gestures to move around in street view:

   - Swipe left or right to turn completely around 360 degrees.

   - Tap farther down the street to move to a different address.

7. Tap the map in the circle to return to map view.

8. Tap the lower-right corner of the screen, which looks like a page about to turn.

9. Tap an option:

   - *Standard* shows a simple street map with street names.

   - *Satellite* shows a photographic image.

   - *Hybrid* mixes the standard and satellite views, showing street names, buildings, parks, and so on.

   - *Terrain* displays a relief map, which isn't such a big deal while looking at a city map. Search for Grand Canyon or Himalayas and it's a lot more interesting.

10. Tap anywhere to return to the map style you were using.

Street View button   Tracking button

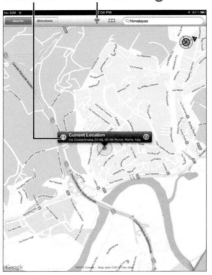

Figure 7-1

Figure 7-2

Searching for an Address or Service

Using Google's search engine, Maps not only finds a specific address that you need but can search by zip code, city, region, or service type. (Do you need a dry cleaner, stat?!) This is one of my favorite Maps features.

Do the following to find an address for someone you know or to find a business or service:

1. Tap the Maps app on the Home screen.

2. Tap the Spotlight search field at the top of the screen. If you see two Spotlight search fields, you're in Directions mode; tap Search at the top left.

3. Type one of the following:

   ■ *An address you want to find, including a street number, city and state, or zip code.*

   ■ *A business or service you seek in an area, for example* Pharmacy *(if you want one near your current location) or* Pharmacy 08230 *(if you want to search another location in a specific zip code).*

   ■ *A neighborhood — for example* Marais Paris *or* North Beach.

4. Tap the Search button on the keyboard.

5. If you searched for a specific address, you see a red pin on the map. The address is written on a flag attached to the pin. If you searched for a business, go to step 6.

6. Tap the List button (on the right of the search field) to see the names and addresses of the results, as shown in Figure 7-3.

List button

Figure 7-3

Finding an Address in Contacts

Maps ties in with Contacts. That way, while you're using Maps, you can tap open a business or person from your Contacts list and search for the location. If you wish to find an address from one of your contacts, follow this sequence:

1. Tap the Maps app on the Home screen.
2. Tap in the Contacts button at the top of the screen, which looks like an open book. Figure 7-4 points out the button. Your Contacts list opens, as shown.
3. Search as you would in Contacts. If you need more information, please read Chapter 5.
   - Scroll through the list.
   - Tap a letter in the index and scroll through that letter.
   - Type the name in the Spotlight search field.
4. When you find what you're looking for, tap it. Maps automatically opens to that address and a pin indicates the location.

To use an address you've recently used, tap the Contacts icon; then tap the Recents button.

Adjusting iPad's location settings and services

When you set up your iPad, I suggest turning on Location Services (unless you'd rather not give your information that way). Maps uses your current or searched-for location to give you the best local information available. If you didn't turn on Location Services while setting up in Chapter 1, you can do so anytime by following these steps:

1. Tap Settings on the Home screen.

2. Tap On for Location Services.

3. Tap On next to Maps.

Contacts button

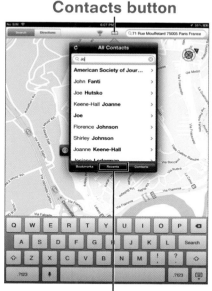

Tap to see recently used addresses

Figure 7-4

Saving and Sharing an Address

The Recents button in Contacts is great for finding an address you sought in the not so distant past. If you keep looking for the same address time and again, however, bookmark it. You can do so even if it's an address that's already in Contacts.

With the same steps outlined in this task, you can create a new contact from Maps or share the address with someone else. Maybe you've found a new restaurant that you really like. You can bookmark the address, add it to Contacts, and share the address with friends, all from Maps.

Here's how to bookmark, save, and share locations from Maps:

1. Tap the Maps app on the Home screen.
2. Tap the Contacts button. Refer back to Figure 7-4 to see the button.

3. Tap the contact you need. Chapter 5 explains in detail how to do this.

4. Tap the pin that indicates your found address.

5. Tap the Information button. It's the white *i* in a blue circle; see Figure 7-5. A window opens with information. A business or service also reveal things like the phone number and website address, as shown in Figure 7-6.

6. Tap the button you want:

   ■ *Add to Contacts* lets you create a new contact or add to an existing contact. Refer to Chapter 5 to read about Contacts.

   ■ *Share Location* lets you send this spot's information to someone via Mail, Messages, or Twitter. (For the latter, you must be logged in to your Twitter account.) Chapters 3 and 4 discuss Mail and Messages, respectively.

   ■ *Add to Bookmarks* lets you edit this location's bookmark.

Information button

Figure 7-5

Figure 7-6

You can create a pin for your current address.

1. Tap the bottom-right corner to show the map options.
2. Tap the Drop Pin button. A purple pin appears on the map.
3. Drag the pin to where you want it. Then you can bookmark and share it.

Asking for Directions

Finding an address is great, but knowing how to get from here to there is really where it's at. You can use Maps to get simple point-A to point-B directions with alternate routes. You can get driving or walking directions, and public transit information is available in some areas.

The walking feature is useful even after the fact: If you've gone for a long stroll, you may want to figure out how many miles you walked.

Follow these steps to have Maps meet your navigation needs:

1. Tap the Maps app on the Home screen.
2. Tap Directions at the top of the screen. The search fields are divided by a squiggly arrow known as the Swap button. Your current location is the starting point. Tap the Swap button to invert the start and end points.
3. Tap in the Start field and type the address from where you want to begin. Or, follow these steps:

    1. Tap the Contacts button (the open book icon).
    2. Tap the Bookmarks, Recents, or Contacts button to find the address.
    3. Tap the address.

4. Tap Directions To Here or Directions From Here, as shown in Figure 7-7.

4. Tap in the End search field and type the address for where you want to wind up.

5. Tap the Search key. The example results are shown in Figure 7-8. I want to go from my current location to the Colosseum.

   ■ The green pin indicates the start point.

   ■ The red pin indicates the end point. Tap the map to close the flag that's attached to the red pin.

   ■ The thick blue line shows the suggested route(s). See Figure 7-8.

   ■ The banner across the bottom shows the means of travel (in Figure 7-8 the car button is active), the route number, travel time, and distance.

6. When you have chosen your preferred route and means of transport, tap Start.

7. Tap the right arrow to see the first indication. The map zooms in on the first item of the directions and the banner gives the instructions, as shown in Figure 7-9. I changed my transport method to walking.

8. Keep tapping the right arrow to see the subsequent steps. Or, tap the Directions button on the left end of the banner to open a list of the step-by-step directions. Tap the Directions button again to close the list. Tap the items in the list to move from one step to the next on the map. You can scroll up and down to see other steps.

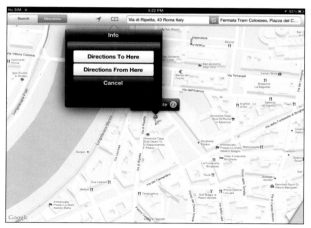

Figure 7-7

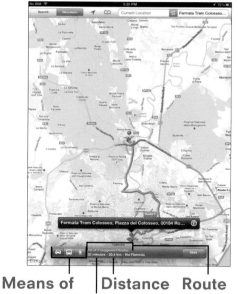

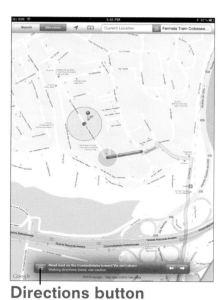

Means of travel   **Distance**   **Route**
                       Travel time **number**

Directions button

Figure 7-8

Figure 7-9

Watching Traffic

Although not available in all areas, when it is available, the Traffic feature in Maps can be a huge timesaver. Shed your doubts: I find it to be quite accurate — more so than traditional radio traffic reports, which seem to mention a traffic jam after it's already cleared. The roads on the map blink with red, yellow, green, or gray highlights to indicate traffic conditions, as shown in Figure 7-10. The example shows a walking route from the Marais neighborhood in Paris to the Mouff'tôt Mouff'tard restaurant. From the looks of the street traffic, walking seems a good idea.

- *Red* means heavy, stop-and-go traffic.
- *Yellow* means traffic is moving below the posted speed limit.
- *Green* means traffic is moving at the posted speed limit.
- *Gray* means there's no traffic information available for that street.

You can see traffic conditions in any of the map views. Do the following to turn it on:

1. Tap the Maps app on the Home screen.
2. Tap the lower-right corner to turn the page and reveal the Maps options.
3. Tap On for the Traffic setting.
4. Tap the screen to return to the map view.

Figure 7-10

Chapter 8

Making Memories with the Camera

Your iPad actually has two cameras: one on the front, where the screen is, and one on the back, and both function as still and video cameras. For the most part, you use the front camera when you want to have a FaceTime conversation or you want to take a picture or video of yourself. (You can also use it as a mirror of sorts, too.) The back camera takes photos and video of things you're looking at, and it has the better quality of the two.

tech to connect

activities

- Taking Photos with Camera
- Recording Video with Camera
- Geotagging
- Stepping Into Photo Booth
- Viewing Your Photos
- Creating Albums and Deleting Photos
- Editing Photos
- Watching and Editing Videos
- Sharing, Printing, or Deleting Photos or Videos
- Using Picture Frame

This is a dense chapter because it presents three apps and a setting that are related to photos. Two apps take photos: Camera, which captures both still images and video, and Photo Booth, which takes photos and has some tricky special effects built in. The third app, Photos, is how you view and edit photos and video. The Picture Frame setting turns your iPad into a digital frame.

The tasks in this chapter take you through taking photos and recording video first, and sprinkled throughout the instructions are tips for improving your photography results and making the most of Camera's features. The fourth task shows you how to use Photo Booth. The remaining tasks discuss the Photos app, where you can view, edit, save, and share the photos and videos you capture with your iPad, and then the last task presents Picture Frame.

Taking Photos with Camera

When you're taking picture with a traditional camera, you probably close one eye and look through the viewfinder. The iPad doesn't have a viewfinder. Instead, you point the iPad at your subject and frame it by looking at the screen. iPad uses face detection, which means it automatically finds and focuses on (up to 10) faces and adjusts the exposure for the best results.

Your iPad has two shutter buttons:

- **Camera button:** Tap the button that appears when you open the Camera app. It looks like a camera (on the right side of the screen). Figure 8-1 points out the button, which changes to a red circle when you switch to video mode.
- **Volume button:** Press the top part of the volume button of your iPad to snap a photo or to start/stop video recording. Be careful not to cover the lens on the back camera when you use the volume button.

Here's how to take a photo with the back camera (with the iPad screen facing you):

1. Tap Camera on the Home screen.
2. Point the iPad at whatever you want to photograph. Rotate the iPad to use portrait or landscape mode.
3. If you see yourself, tap the Switch Camera button at the bottom of the screen.
4. Tap the screen where you want the focus to be. A white square flashes on the screen, indicating where the objective is focused.
5. *Optional:* Tap any dark areas that you want to make brighter.
6. When the on-screen image looks like you want it to, tap the Camera button. Or, press the top part of the Volume button.

   If you have a hard time holding the iPad still, touch and hold the Camera button, steady the camera, and then remove your finger. The photo is taken when you lift your finger.

tech tip

Improving composition with the grid

I have an eye for color but I'm not very good at composition. My landscape photos usually have too much sky and people shots show more body than face. Camera's grid option makes a big difference in balancing out the parts of my photos. You can turn on a grid to make your photo composition even better than it already is. Using what's called the *rule of thirds*, you can place subjects in a way that pleases the eye. The grid helps you visualize the frame in thirds. If the sky fills up the top two-thirds of the grid and the subject is only in the bottom third, you know you should move the iPad to better distribute the sky and subject. Just put your photo's main subject at one of the intersections on the grid and shoot. Follow these steps in the Camera app to turn on the grid: Tap the Options button. Tap On for Grid.

7. Tap the small version (aka thumbnail) to view your photo.

Instead of zooming in on your subject (which you can do by pinching and spreading onscreen), you're better off moving physically closer to take a close-up shot. Getting closer instead of zooming improves the picture quality. If you get *really* close to your subject, about two inches away, macro mode kicks in automatically. Hold your iPad still on the main subject for a few seconds. The main object will be crisp and the background will be blurry, as shown in Figure 8-2.

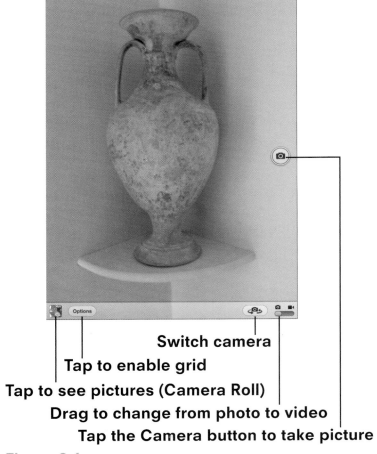

Switch camera

Tap to enable grid

Tap to see pictures (Camera Roll)

Drag to change from photo to video

Tap the Camera button to take picture

Figure 8-1

Figure 8-2

Recording Video with Camera

Holding your iPad to record video might take a little getting used to, but it's worth it. The image quality is superb and with the iPad's built-in video stabilization system, you won't feel seasick when you watch your video. You can re-live great moments like birthday parties, sporting events, and vacations. You can record interviews of your parents and grandparents. Capturing video is similar to taking a photo.

Take these steps to shoot video:

1. Tap Camera on the home screen.
2. Drag the Camera/Video button (refer to Figure 8-1) to video. You have to see something on the screen before you can switch.
3. Point your iPad at the action you want to capture.
4. Tap the Video button or press the Volume Up button. The button is pointed out in Figure 8-3. A single beep means you've started recording. The button blinks while the video is recording.

5. Tap the Video button or press the Volume button to stop recording. A double beep means you've stopped recording.
6. Tap the small image in the bottom left to open the Camera Roll and watch your video.
7. If you don't hear audio with your video, press the Volume button to increase volume output.

If you want to photograph or video yourself, just tap the Switch Camera button to activate the front camera. Capture photos and video the same way as with the back camera, although the front camera has lower resolution, no zoom, and no video stabilization. Tap again to turn the lens around. You'll use it mostly for FaceTime, which I explain in Chapter 4.

Switch Camera button
Camera/Video button
Tap to record (or stop recording)

Figure 8-3

Geotagging

Like a time/date stamp on your photos, geotagging remembers *where* you took the photo or video. This terrific feature saves you from looking at photos and asking "Is that Yellowstone or Yosemite?" You can see a photo's geotag when you view it in Photos, which I explain in this chapter. (Be cautious, though, if you're uploading geotagged photos that you share to a social media site — like Facebook, for example. A photo that says you're at Yosemite tells potential burglars your home is empty.)

To set up geotagging, follow these steps:

1. Tap Settings on the Home screen.
2. Tap Location Services (in the Settings list that runs down the left of the screen).
3. Tap On for Location Services.
4. Tap On for Camera as shown in Figure 8-4.
5. Press the home button to return to the Home screen.

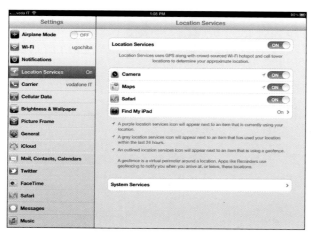

Figure 8-4

Other ways to capture images

You have at least four other ways to capture images on your iPad:

- *Save an image of your screen:* Hold the home button and press the On/Off button at the same time. The shutter clicks and the image is saved to the Camera Roll in Photos.

- *Save from an e-mail:* Tap a photo or video in the message that someone has sent to you. The photo opens in Photos. Tap the Action (arrow) button and then tap Save Image and the photo or video is saved to the Camera Roll in Photos.

- *Capture an image:* From a web page in Safari, tap and hold on an image. Tap Save Image. The image is saved to the Camera Roll album in Photos. Some images may not let you capture them. Do not capture (copy) images from websites without permission from the artist. This is a copyright violation.

- *Use Photo Stream:* If you activate Photo Stream, photos taken with an iPhone or iPod touch or added to iPhoto or Aperture on a Mac connected to iCloud's Photo Stream will be in the Photo Stream album on your iPhone.

Stepping Into Photo Booth

Photo Booth is a fun app that takes photos and adds special effects. You can see the different special effects in Figure 8-5. You can e-mail, copy, or delete the photos directly from the Photo Booth app.

Take a picture, add special effects, and send it to someone with these steps:

1. Tap Photo Booth on the Home screen.
2. If you don't see the special effects chooser, tap the Special Effects button. The special effects chooser, complete with photograph, is shown in Figure 8-5.

Figure 8-5

3. Tap one of the following:
   - Thermal Camera
   - Mirror
   - X-Ray
   - Kaleidoscope
   - Normal (no special effect is applied)
   - Light Tunnel
   - Squeeze
   - Twirl
   - Stretch
4. Tap the Switch Camera button to use either the front camera (to photograph yourself) or the back camera.
5. *Optional:* Drag your finger around the screen and tilt your iPad to create a really special effect — somewhere between Picasso and Dali.

6. Tap the Camera button to take the photo.

7. Tap the thumbnail to view your photo. To send the picture to someone via e-mail, go to step 8. Chapter 3 explains e-mail in more depth.

8. Tap the Action button. The button looks like a rectangle with an arrow, and you can see it pointed out in Figure 8-6.

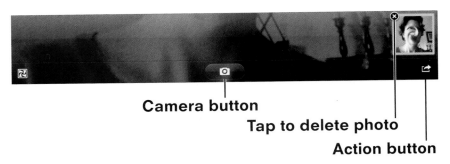

Camera button

Tap to delete photo

Action button

Figure 8-6

9. Tap the photo(s) you want to send. A white arrow in a blue circle indicates the photo(s) you select. Figure 8-7 points them out.

10. Tap one of the following buttons:

   ■ *E-mail* opens a new message with the photo attached. Type in an address and tap Send.

   ■ *Copy* copies the photo, which you can then paste in another app (like Messages, for example).

   ■ *Delete* eliminates the incriminating evidence of the photos. This is a good way to eliminate multiple photos. To eliminate just one photo, tap the X in the corner of the thumbnail.

11. Tap the home button to return to the Home screen.

Indicates chosen photos

Figure 8-7

Viewing Your Photos

Digital photos are no different than printed photos — they beg to be dealt with after you take them. The nice thing about taking photos and videos with your iPad is that you can use your iPad to look at them and show them to other people without any of the mess, inconvenience, and cost: no connecting a cable to a computer, no popping out the memory card, no messing with expensive ink and paper, and no paying for processing.

You create albums in Photos, grouping photos together in a way that makes sense to you. Then, with the slide show feature, your iPad becomes an electronic picture frame. All you need is something to rest it on so your arms don't get tired. (Many of the iPad covers, including Apple's Smart Cover, fold back and become a stand.)

You view your pictures in the Photos app. When you first open the Photos app, you see every picture on your iPad, plus any videos you recorded with it. Six categories sort your photos, as shown in Figure 8-8. You may not see all of the tabs, depending on the types of photos you have stored on your iPad.

- *Photos:* Displays a photo library of all the photos stored on your iPad in chronological order. Tap a photo to open it, and scroll up and down to see more.
- *Photo Stream:* Appears if you have Photo Stream turned on. This shows photos that are in Photo Stream, part of Apple's iCloud remote storage.
- *Albums:* Displays Camera Roll, which is the collection of photos, videos, and screenshots that you capture with your iPad, as well as any album that you create on your iPad or import from a computer or digital camera. Tap an album to see thumbnails of its photos.
- *Events:* Shows groups by the date they were taken. Tap an event to see thumbnails.
- *Faces:* Photos are sorted by identifying people in the photo.
- *Places:* Using geotagging, Photos pins a map to indicate where photos were taken. Tap a pin to open thumbnails of photos taken in that location.

Photo Stream

Photo Stream is part of Apple's iCloud remote storage service. You turn on Photo Stream by tapping Settings and then tapping Photos. When you are connected to Wi-Fi, every time you take a photo or record video with your iPad, Photo Stream automatically sends those images to iCloud. You can put up to 1,000 photos for 30 days on iCloud, but they remain on your iPad unless you delete them. If you use iCloud and Photo Stream with another Apple device (like an iPhone or iPod touch or a Macintosh), Photo Stream downloads the photos to those other devices. Likewise, photos from those other devices go to Photo Stream and to your iPad. For example, if you take photos with a digital camera and then move them to your computer, those photos are uploaded to Photo Stream and downloaded to your iPad.

To view photos, do the following:

- Tap any photo to open and see it in full-screen view. Double-tap with one finger, or pinch and spread with two or three fingers, to zoom in and out. Drag your finger across the screen to move the photo around and see the zoomed parts. Double-tap with two fingers to close the photo.

- Tap a tab, such as Album or Events; then tap the album you want to view. Tap the photo you want to see. Double-tap with two fingers or pinch it to return it to its album. With two or three fingers, pinch the thumbnail view to return to the tab view. (Remember, pinching with four fingers takes you to the Home screen.)

- Swipe from right to left to move to the next photo. Swipe left to right to go back.

- Tap the photo to see the slider shown in Figure 8-9. Drag the slider to see the photo, or tap a photo in the slider.

Tabs

Figure 8-8

You are here   Slider

Figure 8-9

If you have a third-generation iPad, you're in for a spectacular treat: The retina display makes your photos absolutely, beautifully luminous. The iPad 2 has a nice screen too. To view a slideshow on your iPad, regardless of model, follow these steps:

1. Tap Photos on the Home screen.
2. Tap Photos. Or, tap Photo Stream or tap Albums and then tap the album you want to view.
3. *Optional:* Tap a specific photo if you want to begin the slideshow from a photo other than the first one in the library or album.
4. Tap the Slideshow button in the top right. The Slideshow Options screen opens, as shown in Figure 8-10.
5. Tap the Slideshow button in the top right.
6. Tap Transitions. A transition is what happens on the screen between one photo and the next.
7. Tap an option:
   - Dissolve
   - Cube
   - Ripple
   - Wipe
   - Origami
8. Tap Slideshow Options.
9. Tap On for Play Music (if you want to play music, that is). If not, tap Off for Play Music. If you tapped On, go to step 6. If you tapped Off, go to step 7.
10. *Optional:* Tap Music to choose the song you want from your iTunes library. See Chapter 12 for more about iTunes.
11. Tap Start Slideshow.
12. Tap the screen to stop the slideshow.
13. Press the home button to leave Photos.

Maybe you don't like the way things are going in your slideshow. Change the slideshow settings this way:

1. Tap Settings on the Home screen.
2. Tap Photos in the Settings list.
3. Tap Play Each Slide For to change how long each photo stays on the screen. (Maybe you thought the last slideshow went too fast?)
4. *Optional:* Tap On for the Repeat option to play the slideshow continuously (without stopping at the end).
5. *Optional:* Tap On for the Shuffle option to play the photos in a random order.

Figure 8-10

Creating Albums and Deleting Photos

Albums let you group photos together for easy viewing. To create an album on your iPad, follow these steps:

1. Tap the Photos icon on the Home screen.
2. Tap the Albums tab at the top of the screen.
3. Tap the Edit button in the upper right.
4. Tap the New Album button that appears in the upper left.
5. Type a name for your new album. See Figure 8-11.
6. Tap Save. The Add Photos screen shows thumbnails of all the photos on your iPad.
7. Tap all the photos you want in the new album. Scroll down to see more photos.
8. Tap Done.

Figure 8-11

You can add photos to an album any time:

1. Tap the Photos icon on the Home screen.
2. Tap the Albums tab.
3. Tap the album to which you want to add photos.
4. Tap the Action (arrow) button in the upper right. Refer back to Figure 8-6 to see what the button looks like.
5. Tap the Add Photos button.
6. Tap all the photos you want in the new album. Scroll down to see more photos.
7. Tap Done.
8. Tap Albums (in the upper left) to return to the main Photos screen.

tech tip

You can delete photos from an album you create. And even though the photos are removed from the album, they stay in the Photos photo library. If you delete from the Camera Roll album, however, they will be deleted from your iPad completely. Here's how to delete photos:

1. Tap the Photos icon on the Home screen.
2. Tap the Albums tab.
3. Tap the album from which you want to delete photos.
4. Tap the Action (arrow) button. Refer back to Figure 8-6 to see what the button looks like.
5. Tap the photos you want to delete. A checkmark indicates the selected photos.
6. Tap the red Remove button. It's shown in Figure 8-12.
7. Tap Remove From Album to confirm the action.
8. Tap Albums (in the upper left) to return to the main Photos screen.

Figure 8-12

Editing Photos

Your iPad has autofocus and automatically adjusts exposure. No matter. Sometime or another, you'll need to make some corrections. You can correct red-eye, rotate, adjust the color and sharpness, or crop an image.

Follow these steps to edit photos:

1. Tap Photos on the Home screen.
2. Tap the photo you want to edit. You can be in Photos, Photo Stream, an album, or one of the other tabs when you tap the photo.
3. Tap the Edit button.
4. Tap a button:
   - *Rotate* rotates 90 degrees at a time.
   - *Enhance* adjusts the sharpness and contrast.
   - *Red-Eye* requires that you tap the offending eye.
   - *Crop* chops off any unnecessary sides. Use your fingers to zoom, pan, and rotate the image until it looks as you want it to. Drag the corners of the crop grid (see Figure 8-13) to set the area you want to crop. Or, tap the Constrain button to choose one of the preset aspect ratios. Tap Crop.

Drag Corner

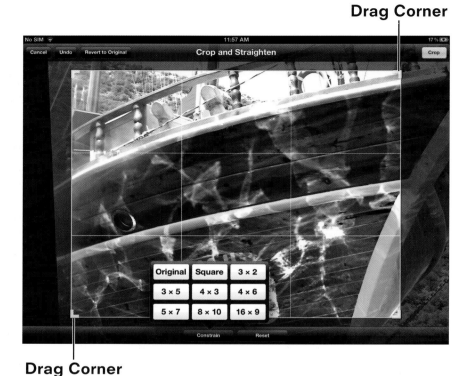

Drag Corner

Figure 8-13

5. *Optional:* If you don't like the edit, tap one of the following:

   ■ *Cancel* leaves edit mode altogether.

   ■ *Undo* undoes the most recent change. Keep tapping to reverse changes one by one.

   ■ *Revert to Original* keeps you in edit mode, but takes your photo back to its original state.

6. When you like the corrections and adjustments you made, tap Save.

7. Tap the Previous button once or twice to return to the main Photos screen. The button will have the name of the album, event, or face, where the photo is stored.

Watching and Editing Videos

After you record video with your iPad, the steps you take to watch it are similar to those you take to view your photos. Photos also lets you trim frames from the beginning and end of the video.

Start recording before the action and let the camera run after you have seen what you want to capture. Then, when you trim off the excess, you always have the full scene you wanted.

The following steps help you watch a video and trim frames. Tap Cancel at any time if you want to start over. Or, tap the Delete (trash can) button any time to simply get rid of the entire video.

1. Tap Photos on the Home screen.
2. Tap the Albums tab.
3. Tap the album where your video is stored. A video icon and playing time stamped on the thumbnail identify a video file.
4. Tap the video you want to watch or edit.

5. Tap the Play button (the triangle). The controls disappear after a few seconds. Tapping the screen reveals them again. To stop playing, go to step 6. To edit a video, go to step 7.
6. Tap the Pause button (or double-tap the screen itself) to stop the video.
7. Tap the far left or right end of the frame viewer. (You might have to tap the screen to see it.) Yellow brackets outline the frame viewer, as shown in Figure 8-14.
8. Tap and hold either yellow bracket. The frames expand.
9. Drag the bracket toward the center. Frames outside the yellow line will be deleted.

10. Tap the Trim button when you have the brackets positioned where you want.

11. Tap an option:

    ■ *Trim Original* saves over the original video. Be careful! This means you won't ever get back the scenes you deleted.

    ■ *Save as New Clip* keeps the original and saves the trimmed video next to the original one in the Camera Roll album.

12. Tap the Play button to watch your edited video.

Frame viewer

Figure 8-14

Sharing, Printing, or Deleting Photos or Videos

Aside from viewing and editing, Photos offers several options for pictures and videos. In addition to sending via e-mail or pasting into another app (explained elsewhere in this chapter), you can do the following with photos:

- Use a photo as the identifying picture for a person or business in Contacts.
- Use a photo as the background wallpaper for your lock and Home screens.
- Print a photo, if you are connected to a printer.

Follow these steps to do one of the actions with one photo or video:

1. Tap Photos on the Home screen.
2. Tap the photo or video you want to use. You can be in the Photos library, in Photo Stream, or in an album.
3. Tap the screen to reveal the controls.
4. Tap the Action (arrow) button to reveal the options shown in Figure 8-15.
5. Tap an option:
   - *E-mail Photo/Video:* Pastes it into a new message. Type in the address and a message if you wish, and tap Send.
   - *Send to YouTube (video only):* Uploads video to your YouTube account. See Chapter 12 for how to do this.
   - *Assign to Contact (photo only):* Assigns the photo to a person or company in Contacts. Choose the contact from the Contacts list that opens. Chapter 5 explains Contacts.

- *Use as Wallpaper (photo only):* Uses the photo as the background for your lock or home screen. Three buttons appear at the top of the screen: Set Lock Screen, Set Home Screen, and Set Both. Tap the button where you want to apply the photo.

- *Tweet (photo only):* Sends your photo to your Twitter account. You must be signed in to Twitter to use this feature.

- *Print (photo only):* Prints the photo. Tap Printer to select an AirPrint-enabled printer that is connected to the same wireless network as your iPad and use the plus and minus signs to choose the number of copies you want to print.

- *Copy Photo/Video:* Creates a copy to paste in another app, such as Messages.

If you want to perform an action on more than one photo or video, you can work with batches. You can use these options when you see photos in the thumbnail view in the Photos photo library, Photo Stream, or in one album at a time (selected from Albums). I think Photos is the easiest place to work from because you can see all the photos on your iPad.

1. Tap Photos, Photo Stream, or the album that has the photos you want to work with.
2. Tap the Action button.
3. Tap the photos or videos you want; they don't have to be consecutive. A white checkmark in a blue circle appears on the photo, as seen in Figure 8-16.
4. Tap a button:

   - *Share:* Tap either E-mail or Print.

tech tip

- *Copy:* You can paste the images in another app, such as Messages.
- *Delete:* Eliminates the selected images. Be careful! If you're in Photos and you delete images that are in albums, the images are deleted from the albums too. If you only want to remove an image from an album, work within the album and tap Remove. See "Creating Albums."
- *Add To:* Tap either Add to Existing Album (then tap the one you want) or tap Add to New Album (then type a name and tap Save).
- *Cancel:* Stops the process.

Action button

Figure 8-15

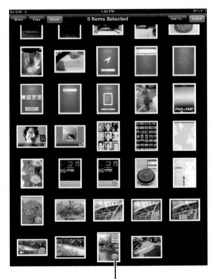

Indicates a selected photo or video.

Figure 8-16

Using Picture Frame

Picture Frame is a fantastic way to take advantage of your iPad's display capabilities. It turns your iPad into a digital picture frame — you may have received one for a gift in the past few years, but I doubt it has the screen quality of your iPad. Also, you can use Picture Frame to see photos even when your iPad is locked or at the Dock.

To set it up, do any of the following you would like. You needn't do all the options — only those you want to change:

1. Tap Settings.
2. Tap Picture Frame to see settings.
3. Tap a transition choice:
   - *Dissolve*
   - *Origami*
4. Tap Show Each Photo For and tap an option. Here is where you change how long each image stays onscreen.
5. Tap On or Off for Zoom In On Faces.
6. Tap On for Shuffle On if you want the photos to appear in random order.
7. Tap the selection of photos you want to see:
   - *All Photos* displays all the photos on your iPad.
   - *Albums* lists all albums; tap the album you want.
   - *Faces* lists people you have identified in Faces; tap the person you want.
   - *Events* lists event groupings; tap the event you want.
8. Tap the home button to close the Settings screen.

9. Press the On/Off Sleep/Wake button on the back of your iPad, at the top right in portrait position.
10. Tap the home button to wake your iPad.
11. Tap the Picture Frame button. The button is pointed out in Figure 8-17. A slideshow starts.

Picture Frame button

Figure 8-17

Chapter 9

Remembering with Calendar

As familial and social circles grow, you have more to remember: birthdays, anniversaries, soccer games, doctor appointments, bridge tournaments, babysitting obligations, luncheons, fundraisers . . . I could go on, but you know what I mean. Add deadlines and expiration dates for taxes, insurance, tire rotations, oil changes, or air conditioner maintenance. Whew! Wouldn't it be nice to have one place for all those dates? This is where iPad's Calendar app comes in.

Calendar has the capacity to be many calendars in one. For example, you can create a car maintenance calendar, a tax calendar, a grandchildren's games calendar, and a medical calendar, and then view them all at once or one at a time. If you use iCloud, you can send invitations to events directly from Calendar.

tech to connect

activities

- Seeing Different Calendar Views
- Adding, Editing, and Deleting Calendars
- Creating Calendar Events
- Changing and Deleting Events
- Searching Calendar
- Sending Invitations from Calendar
- Adjusting Calendar Alert Settings

Some of those tasks might seem over the top. Pick and choose the ones that apply to you. The first tasks in this chapter explain viewing and creating calendars and events. The later tasks tackle more complex activities such as searching Calendar, sending invitations, and adjusting alerts.

Seeing Different Calendar Views

Perhaps you have a monthly calendar hanging on the refrigerator and you refer to it to find out which Sunday is Mother's Day and on what day Fourth of July falls. On the pocket-sized agenda that your bank provided, you jot down doctor and hairdresser appointments. You may have a perpetual calendar that tracks birthdays and anniversaries.

To see the different views in Calendar, do the following:

1. Tap the Calendar app on the Home screen.
2. Tap one of the tabs at the top of the screen:
   - Day
   - Week
   - Month
   - Year
   - List

   Figure 9-1 shows the Day view. If you tap List, you can see all your upcoming events.
3. Move from one day (or week, or month, or year) to the next by doing one of the following:
   - Swipe across the view to move forward or backward one unit at a time. If the page doesn't turn, swipe from the very far edge of the screen.
   - Tap the far left or far right edge of the calendar to move backward or forward one unit.

■ Tap the Backward or Forward button to move one unit into the past or one unit into the future.

4. Tap the Today button to return to the present date in the current view.

In each view, a slider bar at the bottom corresponds to the view. For example, if you're in Day view, the slider shows the days of the month. Tap the day, week, month, or year you want on the slider bar. Drag the slider to the date you want. While your finger is on the slider, the date that corresponds to your finger's position appears in a flag (refer to Figure 9-1), when you lift your finger the calendar screen changes to that date.

Figure 9-1

Adding, Editing, and Deleting Calendars

Calendar lets you create multiple calendars, and each one may have a different theme. If you share your iPad with another person, each person could have her own calendar! You can view these different calendars singly, all together, or some of them together.

Any event that you create in the calendar will be blue. These steps show you how to create a calendar:

1. Tap the Calendar app on the Home screen.
2. Tap the Calendars button in the upper left.

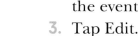

    The Birthdays option, which is under Other, refers to all the birthdays assigned to people in Contacts. Calendar automatically pulls the dates from Contacts and shows them to you if you select Birthdays. The gift icon next to the event means it's a birthday.

3. Tap Edit.
4. Tap Add Calendar. The Add Calendar screen opens.
5. Tap the X in the Untitled Calendar field, where the cursor is blinking.
6. Type a name for the new calendar.
7. Tap a color to assign to this calendar.
8. Tap Done.
9. Repeat steps 4 through 7 to make more calendars.
10. Tap Done to return to the Show Calendars screen.
11. Tap the calendars you want to see on the Show Calendars screen. In Figure 9-2, you can see I've opted to keep my Appointments calendar out of this. Tap Show All Calendars if you want to include events from all your calendars.

These steps show you how to rename and change a calendar's color:

1. Tap the Calendar app on the Home screen.
2. Tap the Calendars button in the upper left.
3. Tap the Edit button in the upper right.
4. Tap in the field where you see Calendar (or one of the other calendars you created previously).
5. Tap the X in the right of the field to delete the word Calendar, as shown in Figure 9-3.
6. Type in a new name. For example, you might use Jilly's Soccer Games or Insurance Due.
7. Tap a color if you want this calendar to be a different color.
8. Tap Done.
9. Tap anywhere on the screen to close the Show Calendars window.

To delete a calendar, follow these steps:

1. Tap the Calendars button.
2. Tap the Edit button in the upper right.
3. Tap the calendar you want to delete.
4. Tap the Delete Calendar button at the bottom of the Edit Calendar screen.

Choose a default calendar — this is where new events will be placed if you don't specify a different calendar.

1. Tap Settings on the Home screen.
2. Tap Mail Contacts, Calendars in the Settings list on the left.
3. Tap Default Calendar in the Calendar section on the right. (Scroll down to find it.)
4. Tap the calendar you want to have as the default.

Calendars that will show

Name field

Tap to delete the name

Figure 9-2

Figure 9-3

Creating Calendar Events

The real power of Calendar is creating events. An event is any item that you put on a calendar. iPad has a Reminders app, but I use Calendar for everything from biweekly classes and dentist appointments to deadlines and the date I have to read the gas meter. Calendar lets you create time-limited events, all-day or multi-day events, and recurring events.

Setting the correct time zone is important if you set alerts for events. The alert will sound at the proper local time. If I've scheduled a FaceTime call with my niece at 11 am Eastern Standard Time, I can type New York in the Time Zone field (introduced in the following steps). If I'm in Rome, the alert for the call will sound at 5 pm there.

Follow these steps to create events:

1. Tap the Calendar app on the Home screen.
2. From any view, tap the plus symbol button in the lower right.
3. Type the name of the event or appointment in the Title field, where the cursor is blinking.
4. *Optional:* Tap in the Location field. Type in an address or whatever else is pertinent.
5. Tap the Starts Ends field. You see a window like the one in Figure 9-4.
6. Tap Start.
7. Scroll to set the date and time the appointment begins.
8. Tap the Ends field.
9. Scroll to set the date and time the appointment ends.
10. If it's an all-day event (for example, your anniversary), tap On for All-Day. If the event is more than one day (a vacation), choose the beginning and ending dates.

11. If the event is in a different time zone, tap Time Zone. If you're not changing the time zone, skip to step 14. (Changing the time zone is optional, but again, if you're setting alarms, make sure this is correctly set. Otherwise, you'll miss your meeting/plane/lunch date.)
12. Type the name of any city in the time zone to which you're going.
13. When you see a city in the time zone, tap it.
14. Tap Done to the Add Event screen.
15. *Optional:* Tap the following fields to add more detail. Tap Done after you complete each field:

■ *Repeat* creates a recurring event. Tap how often the event should repeat. When you choose Every Week or Every 2 Weeks, the event repeats on the day, such as every Tuesday. Tap Every Month or Every Year to repeat the event on the same date. For example, if you set an event on April 9 to repeat monthly, it repeats on May 9, June 9, and so on.

■ *Alert* reminds you of the event — sort of like an alarm clock. Tap when you want to get the alert. Add a second alert if you wish. The alert will sound if the volume is turned all the way down. But if your iPad is muted, the alert doesn't make a sound and you see a visual alert *only* if you have set up Calendar notifications in Settings to do so.

■ *Invitees* (appears only if you have Calendar turned on in iCloud) allows you to invite people to your event. See "Sending Invitations from Calendar."

■ *Calendar* lets you decide on which calendar the event should go (assuming you have more than one).

■ *Availability* helps you avoid scheduling two things at once, especially useful if you use multiple calendars. Tap Busy, and you receive a warning when you try to schedule an appointment at the same time. It also applies to shared calendars.

■ *URL* lets you type a website address.

■ *Notes* lets you type anything you want to remember, such as an address or flight confirmation number. You can copy and paste from other apps to the Notes field in Calendar.

16. Tap Done when you are finished. Refer to Figure 9-5 for a completed event.

Figure 9-4

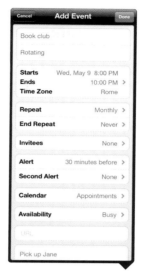

Figure 9-5

Changing and Deleting Events

What's that saying about the best laid plans? Sometimes things go awry; it rains or someone gets the flu. Calendar makes it easy to change or delete events that you created. Just follow these steps:

1. Tap the Calendar app from the Home screen.
2. Tap the event you want to work on.
   - In Day view, the Edit window opens.
   - In Week or Month view, you must tap Edit.
   - In Year view, you must tap the event.

3. To delete an event, tap the red Delete Event button at the bottom of the screen. If you change your mind, tap Cancel. If you simply want to edit the event, not cancel it, follow the same steps described in this chapter's section, "Creating Calendar Events."

4. Tap Done. Figure 9-6 shows example events from different calendars in Week view.

Figure 9-6

Searching Calendar

You know you have *something* to do, *sometime* next week, but you aren't sure what (or when). Search Calendar to locate the day of the event. Calendar searches in the title, location, notes, and invitees fields of calendars that are active — those you have selected in the Calendars list.

Follow these steps:

1. Tap the Calendar app on the Home screen.

2. Tap the Spotlight search field.

3. Type a keyword from the event you want to find. Matches come up as soon as you type, like what you see in Figure 9-7.

4. Tap the event you were searching for. The Event Details screen opens if you're in Day or Year view. An event flag points to the event in Week and Month view. If you don't see what you're looking for, go to step 5.

5. To look at the results again, tap the Search field. To search with new criteria, tap the Search field and tap the X. Repeat steps 3 and 4.

6. Tap an event's Edit button to see more. See Figure 9-8.

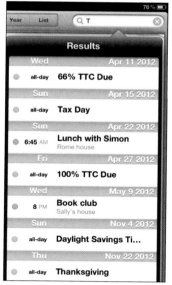

Figure 9-7

Tap to see more info

Figure 9-8

Sending Invitations from Calendar

iCloud is Apple's remote data storage and sharing service that lets you store data from your iPad and, if you have other devices, share information across them — for example, sharing contacts, calendar events, and e-mail between your iPad, desktop computer, and iPhone. Turns out, enabling iCloud lets you use a neat trick in Calendar.

You can send invitations from an event in Calendar to people in Contacts by following these steps:

1. Tap Settings on the Home screen.
2. Tap iCloud in the Settings list on the left.
3. Tap On next to Calendars.
4. Press the home button on the iPad's frame.
5. Tap Calendar on the Home screen.
6. Create an event. You can read how to do that in this chapter.
7. Tap the Invitees field.
8. Tap the plus sign on the right to open Contacts.
9. Tap the person you're inviting. When you're returned to the Add Invitees screen, the name is in the space.
10. Repeat steps 8 and 9 to add more people.
11. Tap Done. An event invitation is automatically sent to your invitees and arrives in their e-mail box. If the invitees use a Calendar-compatible application (such as iCal or Mail) or use another Apple device (such as an iPhone or iPad), the reply goes directly to Calendar when they accept or decline your invitation. In Figure 9-9 you can see I've accepted an invitation.

Head in the iCloud

I admit, I was leery of storing and sharing my data in a "cloud" (sending and storing your data via a wireless connection to a remote site), but I've come to rely on this Apple service for sharing the information I keep in Contacts, Calendar, and Photos between the various devices I use (a Mac, an iPhone, and an iPad). Even if you don't have other devices, iCloud is useful for backing up the information that's on your iPad. I show you how to use iCloud in the bonus chapter titled "Securing Your Data and iPad." You can find the chapter online at `www.wiley.com/go/ipadtechto connect`, although there's enough information here to get started using Calendar and iCloud together.

If you delete an event to which you had invited people, an e-mail is automatically sent to all invitees. It lets them know the event has been cancelled. That sure saves a lot of phone calls!

Figure 9-9

Adjusting Calendar Alert Settings

You can set an alert, which is sort of like an alarm clock — both get you going. Setting up alerts is something you have to do just once, unless you want to change the settings or sound.

Follow these steps to set an alert or change the notification style:

1. Tap Settings on the Home screen.
2. Tap Notifications in the Settings list.
3. Tap Calendar in the Notifications list.
4. Tap one of the options shown in Figure 9-10:

   Notification Center: Tap On to see Calendar alerts in the Notification Center.

   Alert Style: Tap the alert style you prefer: None, Banner, or Alert. Banners just go across the top of your iPad screen; alerts are a better option.

Don't like the way your alert sounds? Follow these steps to change it:

1. Tap Settings on the Home screen.
2. Tap General in the Settings list on the left.
3. Tap Sounds in the General list on the right.
4. Tap Calendar Alerts in the list.
5. Tap an alert tone to hear what it sounds like.
6. When you find one you like, tap it. A checkmark indicates this is your choice. This sound will alert you to an upcoming event.

If you choose None, only visual alerts set in the Notification Center will appear on the screen. If you choose None for both the sound *and* the Alert Style in the Notification Center, you won't see an alert even if you asked for an alert for a specific event.

If the volume is turned all the way down but you have assigned a sound alert, the alert will still sound. If, however, your iPad is muted, the alert doesn't make a sound. You will see a visual alert *only* if you have set up Calendar notifications in Settings to do so.

Follow these steps to set up a default alert time for specific types of recurring events:

1. Tap Mail, Contacts, Calendars in the Settings list on the left.
2. Scroll down and tap Default Alert Times in the Calendar section.
3. Tap Birthdays.
4. Tap when you want to get an alert for birthdays. The options are shown in Figure 9-11.
   - On Day of Event
   - 1 Day Before
   - 2 Days Before
   - 1 Week Before
5. Tap the Default Alert Times button.
6. Tap Events.
7. Tap when you want to receive an alert for events.
8. Tap the Default Alert Times button.
9. Tap All-Day Events.
10. Tap how soon *before* an all-day event you want to receive an alert:
    - 15 minutes
    - 1 hour
    - 2 days
11. Press the home button on the iPad frame to return to the Home screen.

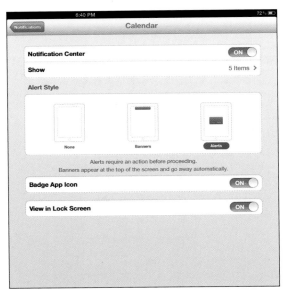

Figure 9-10

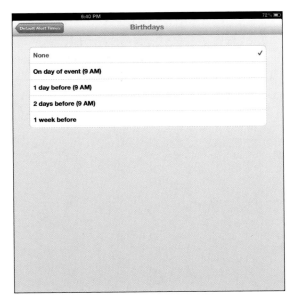

Figure 9-11

Chapter 10

Shopping for Music, Movies, Books, Apps, and More

It seems odd to have a chapter dedicated to how to shop, but that's what you find outlined in the tasks here. Maybe you're familiar with online shopping; shopping in the iTunes and App Stores isn't that different. If, on the other hand, your iPad is your first time electronic shopping, it takes a little getting used to. In the iTunes or App Stores, you just tap your way to the item you desire. Each Apple storefront looks similar. Once you understand how to find your way through the virtual aisles of one store, you'll feel right at home browsing through the others.

tech to connect

activities

- **Shopping at the iTunes Store**
- **Buying Movies and TV Shows from iTunes**
- **Shopping at the App Store**
- **Updating Apps**
- **Deleting Apps**
- **Reinstalling Apps You Already Own**

tech tip

No matter which store you visit, make sure you have your Apple ID and password, and either a credit card or an iTunes or Apple gift card to pay. Chapter 1 helps you create an Apple ID if you haven't already.

This chapter explains how to find and download media from iTunes and the App Store. I show you, step by step, how to locate other media you may want, how to buy it, and then how to download it. The last tasks explain how to manage apps that you purchase. Chapter 12 explains how to listen to or watch the media your download.

Shopping at the iTunes Store

The iTunes store, which appears as just iTunes on your iPad's Home screen, is a one-stop media shopping wonderland: music, movies, TV shows, podcasts, and audiobooks. You browse the iTunes store and then download media. Some of it is free and some of it is not. For example, podcasts (which are free over-the-air shows) and many sneak previews for new television series are free. You can rent or buy movies; you can buy music by song, or you can buy the whole album. iTunes also puts together special music collections by artist or genre.

Podcasting

I'm curious by nature but have neither the time nor the inclination to study in-depth all the things that interest me. So I listen to audio podcasts or watch video podcasts to get an introduction to new topics, listen to my favorite radio programs from NPR, and watch Mark Bittman make potato pizza. Many of your favorite news commentators and comedians may have their own podcasts, and there's even a *Sesame Street* podcast if you need to keep a little one occupied for a bit. Best of all, podcasts are free.

This store has so many options that I've listed them here. At the top of the screen you can see these options:

- *Genres:* Music, movie, or TV show genres. The button changes to *Categories* when you are looking at podcasts or audiobooks. The Genres list opens, as shown in Figure 10-1.
- *Featured:* Thumbnails of media chosen by the iTunes editors. The section names change but one section usually highlights new releases and another highlights seasonal releases (for example, baseball songs) or music style (such as a guitarists section in the Blues genre).
- *Top Charts:* This features bestsellers. Choosing a genre here helps you narrow the options. Figure 10-2 shows the top movies in the Classic genre.
- *Genius:* The iTunes Store makes recommendations based on your past purchases and media that's already on your iPad. Genius won't work until you download media. This option appears in Music, Movies, and TV Shows.
- *Spotlight search:* Tap in this field and then type the item you're looking for. A list of results appears and narrows as you type more letters. When you find what you want, tap it to open the selection.

Or, you can tap a media type at the bottom of the screen:

- Music
- Movies
- TV Shows
- Podcasts
- Audiobooks
- iTunes U

You can tell which media type you're viewing by the button that is highlighted at the bottom of the screen. The buttons that are grayed at the top indicate the genre or category you're viewing.

Figure 10-1

Figure 10-2

1. Tap iTunes on the Home screen to open the store. It will look similar to what you see in Figure 10-3.

Sections

Collections

Figure 10-3

2. Tap an option.
3. Tap an image that interests you. The album information window opens. Figure 10-4 shows my selection: a Diana Krall album.
4. *Optional:* Tap a number next to one of the songs to hear a sample.
5. Tap the price next to a song to buy one song. Or, tap the price under the album name to buy the entire album. The button changes to read Buy Song or Buy Album. If an item is free, the button reads Free.
6. Tap the Buy (or Free) button.
7. Type your Apple ID and password. Free items begin downloading immediately.

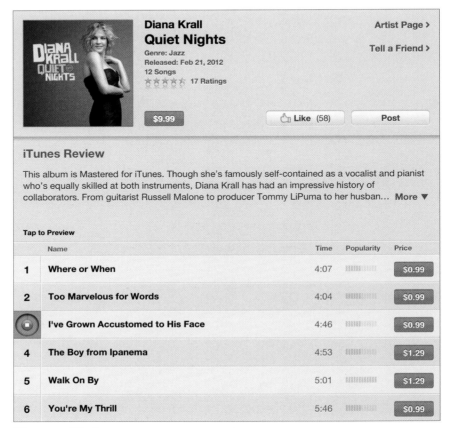

Figure 10-4

8. Type your credit card information into your Apple ID account. *If you're redeeming an Apple or iTunes gift card, skip to the set of steps that follow these.*

9. Scroll down to the bottom of the iTunes screen.

10. Tap the Sign In button. You can see the button in Figure 10-5.

11. Tap Use Existing Apple ID.

12. Type your Apple ID and password.

13. Scroll down to the bottom again and tap AppleID: *yourAppleID.*

14. Tap View Apple ID.
15. Tap Payment Information. The Account Settings screen opens.
16. Tap the type of credit card you want to use.
17. Tap the Card Number field and type your number.
18. Tap the Security Code field and type your number.
19. Tap the Month field and Year field to select the expiration date.
20. Tap in the Bill Address field and then tap in the Phone Number field and type in your information.
21. Tap Done to return to the Account Settings window.
22. Tap Done again to return to iTunes.

Tap here

Figure 10-5

If you're redeeming a gift card at the iTunes Store, follow these steps:

1. Tap iTunes on the Home screen.
2. Find what you want to buy.
3. Tap the price next to a song or tap the price under the album name.
4. Tap the Buy button.
5. Type your Apple ID and password.
6. Scroll down to the bottom of the iTunes screen. Refer to Figure 10-5.
7. Type in the code from the card or certificate.
8. Type in your Apple ID and password (if you aren't signed in to your account). The amount of the card is added to your account and appears next to your name.
9. Tap Done to return to the Account Settings window.
10. Tap Done again to return to iTunes.

Tap the Purchased button at the bottom of the screen to see the items you purchased. Personally, I find it easier to pick up an iTunes card at the grocery store and redeem it on iTunes instead of using a credit card.

Buying Movies and TV Shows from iTunes

iTunes may have been just for music at the beginning but now it is a veritable storehouse of media, not the least of which are movies and TV shows. Most movies and television shows are available in both high definition (HD) and standard definition (SD) format. The screen on your iPad takes full advantage of HD video and, although it does cost more than SD, the difference in quality is noticeable. You can rent or buy movies can be rented or purchased. You can buy TV shows by episode or by the season, with new episodes automatically downloaded when released.

Whether you buy or rent a movie or TV show, a number on the Downloads button in the bottom right indicates the number of items you are downloading. Tap the Downloads button to see how long it will take to download the item. Your downloading item appears in a list. The file size and download time appear under the title.

Chapter 12 picks up where these steps leave off. If you want to watch your movie or show, go there after following these steps. Do the following to buy or rent and then download a movie:

1. Tap the iTunes app on the Home screen.
2. Tap Movies at the bottom of the screen.
3. Tap an option, depending on where you want to start looking:
   - Genre
   - Featured
   - Top Charts
4. Tap a movie. The information window opens, as shown in Figure 10-6.
5. *Optional:* Tap Preview to see a trailer.

6. Tap HD or SD. These options indicate the movie quality. HD is high definition and looks great on the third-generation iPad. SD is standard definition and usually costs a few dollars less than HD. When I'm renting a movie, I usually go with SD. If I buy a movie, I prefer HD since it's something I plan to watch more than once and I appreciate the better quality image.
7. Tap Buy or Rent.
8. Tap Buy Movie or Rent Movie.
9. Type in your Apple ID and password.
10. Tap OK. The movie begins downloading.
11. Tap outside the window to close it.

Do the following to buy and download a TV show:

1. Tap iTunes on the Home screen.
2. Tap TV Shows at the bottom of the screen.
3. Tap an option, depending on where you want to start looking:
   - Genre
   - Featured
   - Top Charts
4. Tap a TV Show. The information window opens as shown in Figure 10-7.
5. Tap HD or SD. These options indicate the image quality as explained in the previous instructions.
6. Tap an option:
   - Buy (under the title; this lets you buy a season pass)
   - Buy (next to an episode; this lets you buy only that episode)
7. *Optional:* Preview an episode by tapping the playback button to the left of the episode description.
8. Tap Buy Season or Buy Episode.
9. Type in your Apple ID and password.
10. Tap OK. The TV show begins downloading.
11. Tap outside the window to close it.

Tap Featured while you're viewing one of the categories: Music, Movies, or TV Shows. Scroll down to the bottom of the screen to see the Quick Links section. There are buttons you can tap for free and discounted music, movies, and TV shows; refer back to Figure 10-5.

Elizabeth: The Golden Age PG-13 HD   Tell a Friend >

Working Title
Genre: Drama
Released: 2008
1080p HD
★★★★☆ 185 Ratings

PREVIEW

BUY $14.99   RENT $3.99   HD   SD

Learn About Rentals >

Plot Summary

Academy Award® winners Cate Blanchett and Geoffrey Rush join Academy Award® nominee Clive Owen in a gripping historical thriller full of suspense, intrigue and adventure! When Queen Elizabeth's reign is threatened by ruthless familial betrayal and Spain's invading army, s... **More ▼**

Credits

Actors	Director	Screenwriters	Producers
Cate Blanchett >	Shekhar Kapur >	Michael Hirst >	Tim Bevan >
Geoffrey Rush >		William Nicholson >	Eric Fellner >
Clive Owen >			Jonathan Cavendish >
Rhys Ifans >			
Jordi Molla >			
Abbie Cornish >			

Figure 10-6

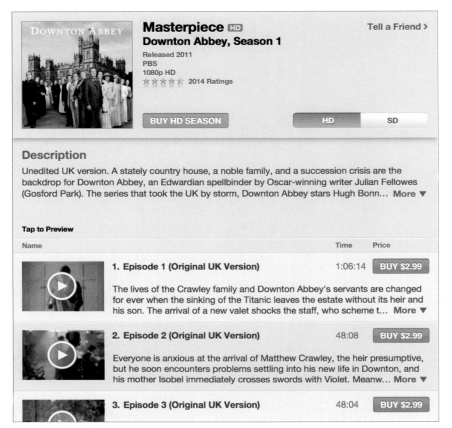

Figure 10-7

Shopping at the App Store

Apps, short for *applications*, add lots of capabilities to your iPad. Your iPad comes to you with great apps (such as Messages, Calendar, Maps, and Camera), and this book explains how to use them. But that's not all. The App Store has hundreds of thousands of more apps available. Many are free and most are inexpensive. The App Store offers one-stop shopping so you don't have to search all over the web for the best price or the latest version; everything is in one place.

The App Store is similar to the iTunes store. The buttons at the bottom of the screen offer other ways to view apps:

- *Featured* groups apps by date (such as New & Noteworthy) or popularity (such as Staff Favorites).
- *Genius* makes suggestions based on apps you already own.
- *Top Charts* classifies apps by the most downloaded paid and free apps and the apps that have earned the most money.
- *Categories* lets you view apps by a specific category such as Books, Games, Finance, or Health and Fitness.

- *Purchased* shows a list of the apps you've bought. This list is tied to your Apple ID and is useful if you lose your iPad or upgrade to a new one.
- *Updates* shows a number if updates are available for the apps you have installed on your iPad. Tapping Updates automatically opens a list of apps and you can choose to update all or some.

Do the following to buy an app from the App Store:

1. Tap the App Store button on the Home screen. The first time you open the App Store, a message asks if you want to download your free copy of iBooks, as shown in Figure 10-8. You can tap Not Now.
2. Tap one of the tabs (at the top of the screen) or one of the buttons at the bottom and search for what you are looking for:
   - *New* reveals the most recently released apps.
   - *What's Hot* shows you the most frequently downloaded apps.
   - *Release Date* shows all the apps, which may be sorted by release date, most popular, or name.
   - *Spotlight Search* results are based on what you type in the search field.

3. Tap the app. You will see some details.

4. If you know what app you want, tap the Free or *Price* button, which is shown in Figure 10-9. Or, tap the app and read the app description carefully. (It's easy to download something only to find it isn't what you wanted.)

5. Tap the Install App or Buy App button. See Figure 10-9.

6. Type your Apple ID and password.

7. Tap OK.

8. As with iTunes, if you are buying an app, you must use a credit card or an Apple or iTunes gift card to pay.

The button reads *Installing* and changes to *Installed* when the download is complete. If you press the home button, you see a dim version of the app icon with the word *Loading* and a progress bar. How long it takes to download depends on the size of the app. Most apps take a minute or two. They download one at a time, so if you download several at once, they will wait their turn.

Both the App Store and iTunes store keep a record of everything you download. This means if your iPad breaks or you replace it with a newer model, you can download your apps and media again — without paying for them a second time. That's one reason you sign in with your Apple ID even for items that are free.

Apps-olutely

I download a lot of apps — especially free ones — but I do have my favorite paid apps (StarWalk identifies the constellations and Angry Birds is a game that demands acute slingshot skills.) Some of the free apps I use frequently are my bank, Lufthansa, Apple's iBooks, and iTunes U. When you download free apps, be aware that some apps *seem* free but only provide a portion of what the paid app can do. Or, a free app may have advertisements, whereas the paid version is ad-free. Again, it's your choice.

Figure 10-8

Tap to begin a purchase

Figure 10-9

To find other apps, tap through Categories or Top Charts. When you see an app that interests you, tap it and read through the Info screen. Tap Free or the *Price* button to download the app. Both require your Apple ID; purchased apps will require a credit card, an App Store credit, or gift card number associated with your Apple ID.

Updating Apps

Eventually, a white number in a red circle will appear on the shoulder of the App Store button on the Home screen; see Figure 10-10. That's when you know you have apps to update. The number indicates how many apps have updates, and the same number, known as a *badge*, appears on the Updates button in the bottom-right corner of the Apps Store app. An update is almost always an improvement (usually to fix problems). The App Store automatically checks for updates once a week, and also looks for updates whenever you sign in. It doesn't cost you anything to get an update.

Although the badge on the App Store button indicates available updates, some apps let you know within the app when a new version is available. You might be playing a game and a notification appears, telling you that a new version is available. Simply tap the link that appears. There may be a fee involved if it's an *upgrade*, say from a barebones free version to a paid-for full version. You can decide against that if you prefer not to pay.

You can update one app at a time or update all the apps at once:

1. Tap App Store on the Home screen.
2. Tap the Updates button on the bottom-right corner of the App Store.
3. Tap the app in the list to see what was changed.
4. Tap the Update button on the info screen. Or, tap Update All. See Figure 10-11.

If for some reason the download is interrupted, the download starts again the next time you have an Internet connection.

Badge shows that 10 updates are ready

Figure 10-10

Tap here to update all apps at once

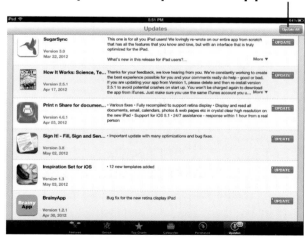

Figure 10-11

Deleting Apps

Sometimes you download an app and it just doesn't meet your needs, or worse yet, it wreaks havoc on your iPad — the keyboard freezes every time you open it or the screen stops responding. You can delete it from your iPad. If you accidentally delete an app from your iPad, you can download it again from the App Store. You can't, however, delete the apps that came with your iPad.

To delete apps, do the following:

1. Press and hold any app on the Home screen until all the apps start wiggling.
2. Tap the X in the corner of the app you want to delete. You can see the X in Figure 10-12.
3. Press the home button when you're finished to make the app icons stand still.

Tap an X to delete an app

Figure 10-12

Reinstalling Apps You Already Own

Remember the app you deleted because it wasn't quite right? If you're feeling nostalgic for an app that you deleted, or you replaced your old iPad with a newer model, you can reinstall the apps you previously downloaded. The App Store keeps track of apps you already bought and lets you download them again (if they're still available from the App Store), free of charge. Follow these steps:

1. Tap App Store on the Home screen.
2. Tap the Purchased button at the bottom of the screen. A list appears, and looks similar to the one in Figure 10-13.
3. Tap the Not On This iPad button.
4. Tap the Download button (cloud with an arrow). You can see it in Figure 10-13.
5. Type in your Apple ID and password, if requested.
6. Click OK.

Download button

Figure 10-13

Chapter 11

Reading Up on Newsstand, iBooks, and iTunes U

You probably noticed how brilliant the iPad display is, especially if you have a third-generation iPad. Newsstand, one of my favorite apps, turns your iPad into an electronic magazine or newspaper. If you commute or travel (and read) a lot, Newsstand is a great alternative to lugging *The New York Times*, *The Economist*, and *National Geographic* on a train, bus, or plane. What's more, Newsstand gives you access to publications that might be tough to find at your local newsstand — publications like the *British Journal of Photography*, *Thanh Nien News*, *Adrenalin DE*, and a slew of foreign newspapers and magazines. And then there are all the books available for the iPad!

tech to **connect**

activities

- **Downloading the App and Subscribing**
- **Reading Magazines and Newspapers from Newsstand**
- **Stocking Your iBooks Shelves**
- **Reading an E-book**
- **Organizing Your E-books**
- **Making the Grade at iTunes U**

The first tasks in this chapter explain subscribing to and reading newspapers and magazines in Newsstand, which is pre-loaded on your iPad. The next tasks are all about iBooks, which is both a bookstore and an electronic reader app — also pre-loaded. The last task shows you how to enroll in iTunes U, which brings together lectures and courses from various universities worldwide and gives you access to lessons from K-12 institutions and presentations and video.

Downloading the App and Subscribing

Each periodical has an app to download. The periodical apps go in your Newsstand bookshelf. The app is (usually) free, but you *buy* a subscription or an issue of the newspaper or magazine. After you download the publication's app and see it in Newsstand, you can buy and download magazines or newspapers. A yearly subscription is often much more convenient and economical than buying individual issues. If you subscribe to the print version of a magazine or newspaper, odds are you can access it for free on your iPad.

Before you start, make sure you have your Apple ID and password, as well as your credit card, ready. Follow these steps to find and download a magazine or newspaper subscription:

1. Tap Newsstand on the Home screen.
2. Tap Store in the upper-right corner of the Newsstand folder.
3. Tap an option (at the bottom of the screen) to see periodicals sorted a certain way:
   - *Featured* shows new and recommended publications.
   - *Genius* gives you recommendations based on your past purchases.

- *Top Charts* shows best-selling publications.
- *Categories* sorts publications by group, as shown in Figure 11-1.
- *Spotlight search* field appears in any of these views. Tap the field and type the name of a publication.

4. Tap the magazine icon.

5. Tap the Free button or *Price* (under the icon) shown in Figure 11-2. You are downloading the app so you can get a subscription or single issue.

6. Tap Install App.

7. Tap the app icon in Newsstand to go back and subscribe.

8. Tap one of the following, which are shown in Figure 11-3:

   - *Buy* gets you a single copy. Tap OK or Confirm. Then type your Apple ID and password. The issue is downloaded. Tap the icon to see a description and table of contents before buying.

   - *Subscribe* starts a subscription. If more than one kind is available, tap the one you want. Particularly with dailies, one- or three-month subscriptions are available. Type your Apple ID and password to pay from your iTunes Store account. The current issue is downloaded.

   - *Download* automatically puts a free or sample issue on your iPad.

9. Tap OK when asked if you would like to be sent new issues and push notifications. This means you'll get the publications as they are released. Updates happen only when you are connected to Wi-Fi.

10. Tap View to read the issue.

If you subscribe to the print version of the publication, tap the Support or FAQ button to see what you need to get to your subscription on the iPad. It may just be your name and address, or you might need the subscription number from the mailing label.

Figure 11-1

Tap here

Figure 11-2

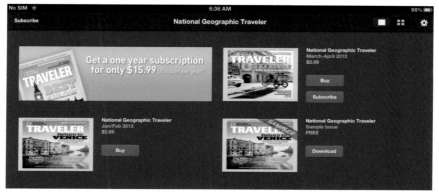

Figure 11-3

Reading Magazines and Newspapers from Newsstand

tech tip

A badge appears on the Newsstand app when a publication you get releases a new issue, and the publication app wears a *New* banner.

When you want to read a periodical from Newsstand, follow these steps:

1. Tap Newsstand on the Home screen. You'll see those periodicals to which you're subscribed. My Newsstand looks like Figure 11-4.
2. Tap the icon for the periodical you want to read.
3. Tap the issue you want to read (if there is more than one).

Use the following gestures to read a magazine. Chapter 1 describes gestures more fully:

- *Swipe* to turn pages or move from article to article.
- *Scroll* to move up and down on a page. There's usually an arrow in the lower right to indicate that the article continues on the same screen.

- *Tap* items in the table of contents to go to that article.

- *Tap* the screen to reveal command buttons at the top and bottom of the screen, as shown in Figure 11-5. Icons vary slightly, but here are a few guidelines:

  - A button that looks like vertical lines changes from a single page to thumbnail images of the entire issue. Tap the thumbnail to open a page; tap Done to go back to the single page.

  - A button that looks like horizontal lines opens the table of contents.

  - The Library button sometimes looks like a house; sometimes it's labeled Store. Tap it to see all the available issues of that publication. In this view, two buttons in the top right switch between a single issue and multi-issue view.

  - Tap the Share button (rectangle with an arrow) to send a link to the article you're reading. You will send the link via e-mail or post it on your Facebook or Twitter account. Tap the option you want.

Use these gestures to read a newspaper, one of which is shown in Figure 11-6:

- *To open the full version:* Tap a headline or article.

- *To open a section:* Tap the Sections button, and then tap an item, such as Politics, World News, or Sports.

- *To return to the front page from an article:* Tap the X or Top News button.

To rearrange or delete the publication apps on the Newsstand shelf, touch and hold one app until they all wiggle. Touch and drag the icon to a new position or tap the X to delete the publication app. Be careful! If you delete the publication app, you won't be able to read any issues you received.

Figure 11-4

Tap to see all the publications issues
Tap to share
Tap to go to table of contents

Tap to change view

Figure 11-5

Figure 11-6

Stocking Your iBooks Shelves

iBooks is an app that lets you read e-books and documents in ePUB or PDF formats. You may be hesitant to replace your traditional ink-on-paper books for e-books. Why e-not try it? The iBookstore gives you plenty of choices for your first e-book and many are free (especially all those classics that, if you're like me, you haven't gotten around to reading yet). You can also get free e-books from your public library, `http://books.google.com`, and Project Gutenberg (at `www.gutenberg.org`). For more on this, see *AARP Tablets: Tech to Connect*.

Before you start, make sure you have your Apple ID and password ready. The book you decide on may be free, but have your credit card ready just in case.

Follow these steps to shop in the iBookstore:

1. Tap iBooks on the Home screen.

2. Tap Store in the upper left. The iBookstore opens, as shown in Figure 11-7.

Section

Collections

Figure 11-7

3. Tap the following to look:

   ■ *See All* to view all the books in a section.

   ■ *Icons* between the sections to view collections (such as baseball books or books for $3.99 or less).

   ■ *New York Times* for the bestseller lists.

   ■ *Top Charts* to see iBooks' most downloaded paid and free books.

- *Categories* to choose a specific genre from which to view available books.

  - *Browse* to see authors alphabetically. Tap to view by category and paid/free books.

4. Tap the book that interests you.

5. Tap the Free or *Price* button under the book image.

6. Tap Buy Book or Get Book. Or, tap the Get Sample button to download a sample chapter of a book. You can see if you like it and then download the entire book.

7. Type in your Apple ID and password.

8. Tap OK to download the book. The book will look like what you see in Figure 11-8, with the New banner (until you tap to open it).

This icon appears until you open your e-book the first time

Figure 11-8

Reading an E-book

Reading an e-book on your iPad is about as simple as reading a paperback book, although the iPad offers an advantage: You can adjust the type size and take notes without messing up the pages. Some books even have a read-aloud option.

If you want to read in bed, use the orientation lock so the screen doesn't rotate when you lie down. Double-tap the Home button, swipe the open apps bar to the right, and tap the orientation lock button.

Use these gestures to get around in an e-book:

- Tap the right edge of the screen to turn the page.
- Tap the left edge of the screen to go back a page.
- Tap the screen to reveal the on-screen controls. Drag the slider at the bottom of the screen to get to a page. Tap the screen again to hide the on-screen controls.
- Tap the Contents button in the upper left (pointed out in Figure 11-9; it looks like three exclamation points on their right sides) to see the table of contents.
- Tap any item in the table of contents to jump to that page.

All of these steps are optional. For example, if the screen brightness is just fine, skip that step. Here are the steps for making an e-book easier on your eyes:

1. Tap iBooks on the Home screen.
2. Tap the book you want to read.
3. Tap any page.
4. Tap the Type Size button (aA). This function works only with ePUB-format books. You can zoom in on PDF documents to enlarge the image, but you can't change the type size.

5. Drag the slider left or right to change the brightness of the screen.

6. Tap the smaller a or larger A to change the type size.

7. Tap the Fonts button.

8. Tap the font you want to use.

9. Tap the Theme button.

10. Tap one of the contrast options:

    ▪ Normal (black letters on a white background)

    ▪ Sepia (dark-gray letters on an off-white background)

    ▪ Night (white letters on a black background)

11. Tap On for the Full Screen switch to use the entire screen for the page.

12. Tap the e-book page to return to reading.

13. Tap the Library button to return to the iBooks shelf.

You can perform these tasks also:

▪ *Look for a word or page number in the book.* Tap the Search button (pointed out in Figure 11-9) and type your criteria.

▪ *Remember a specific page you want to come back to later.* Tap the Bookmark button. (You don't have to do this when you close iBooks. It will remember where you stopped reading and open to that page the next time you open the book.)

▪ *Copy or highlight a word.* Touch a word; options appear when you lift your finger. Drag the grabbers to highlight the part of the text you want to copy, highlight, or underline, and then tap Copy or Highlight.

▪ *See a word's definition.* Touch a word and lift your finger. Tap Define. To search the entire web for a definition, tap Search Web. Refer to Figure 11-10.

▪ *Type something related to the highlighted text.* Tap Note to bring up a tag in the margin. You can see your notes and highlighted text in the Notes section of the table of contents.

- *Delete a highlight or note.* Tap the highlighted section and tap the circle/slash to delete the highlight. Delete the text in the note to make it disappear.

A button that looks like a speaker indicates the book has audio capabilities. Tap the button to hear the book read aloud.

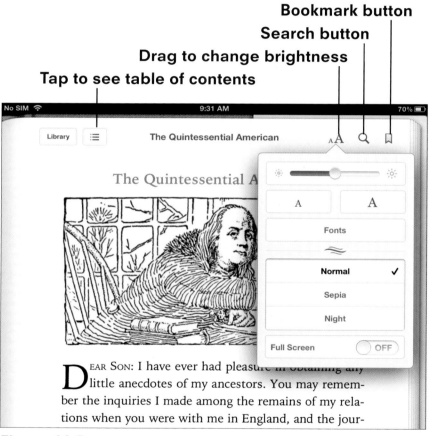

Figure 11-9

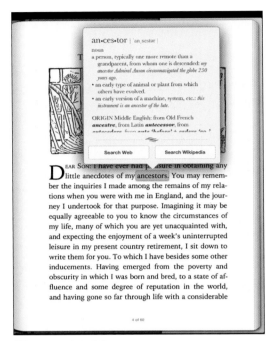

Figure 11-10

E-reader convert

I tried e-readers, but the iPad actually did the trick. Since the iPad already serves so many other purposes for me, its e-reader functionality is a bonus rather than the raison d'être. Plus, I can get and share so many good books from sources such as Baen Ebooks (www.baenebooks.com) and Project Gutenberg (www.gutenberg.org).

Organizing Your Books

If you have a dozen or so books, you can see them on one screen. It doesn't take long to amass a library that's close to breaking the shelves. iBooks adds shelves as needed, and you can use the Spotlight search at the top of the shelf. Still, it's nice to organize your reading materials, no?

Follow these steps to organize your library:

1. Tap iBooks on the Home screen.
2. Tap the Collections button.
3. Tap New.
4. Type a name for a group of books you have. An author or genre is a good group (for example, Biographies or John Irving).
5. Tap Done.
6. Tap the Edit button.
7. Tap the books you want to place in the collection you just created. A checkmark appears on selected books, like you can see in Figure 11-11.
8. Tap Move.
9. Tap the collection into which you want to place the book(s).
10. Swipe left and right to move between collections.

To rearrange the books on the shelves, tap and hold a book until it gets slightly bigger, and then drag it to a new position. The other books move to make room for it.

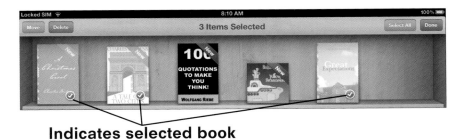

Indicates selected book

Figure 11-11

Making the Grade at iTunes U

iTunes U is how you can study Hebrew scriptures at Harvard, Shakespeare at Oxford, computer science at Stanford, and economics at Berkeley — without ever paying tuition. This time, however, you don't have exams or term papers — just the enjoyment of learning from some of the best minds at the most respected and prestigious universities in the world. You can attend one lecture or an entire semester.

Chapter 10 tells you how to install the iTunes U app.

You can look for courses in various ways once you get into the following steps:

- *Featured* shows the newest courses.
- *Top Charts* shows the most popular courses.
- *Categories* shows subjects, including Business, Fine Arts, Language, and Science. Tap the category to see courses.
- The *Spotlight search field* lets you type an institution name or subject.

Here's how to enroll in iTunes U:

1. Tap iTunes U on the Home screen.
2. Tap the Catalog button in the upper left.
3. Tap an option:
   - *Universities & Colleges* offers university courses. See Figure 11-12.
   - *Beyond Campus* offers lectures and presentations from non-academic associations, museums, and libraries.
   - *K-12* offers lessons from elementary through high-school curricula.

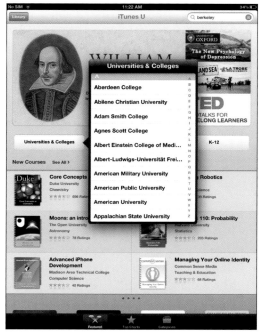

Figure 11-12

4. Tap a course that interests you.

5. Tap the number next to the lecture to see a preview. I tapped Materials to see the list shown in Figure 11-13.

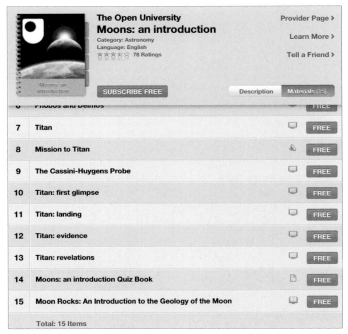

The Open University
Moons: an introduction
Category: Astronomy
Language: English
★★★☆☆ 78 Ratings

Provider Page ›
Learn More ›
Tell a Friend ›

SUBSCRIBE FREE   Description | Materials (15)

6	Phobos and Deimos		FREE
7	Titan		FREE
8	Mission to Titan		FREE
9	The Cassini-Huygens Probe		FREE
10	Titan: first glimpse		FREE
11	Titan: landing		FREE
12	Titan: evidence		FREE
13	Titan: revelations		FREE
14	Moons: an introduction Quiz Book		FREE
15	Moon Rocks: An Introduction to the Geology of the Moon		FREE

Total: 15 Items

Figure 11-13

6. Tap Subscribe Free (under the title) to download the entire course. Or, tap the Free button next to one of the lectures. The button changes to Get Course or Get Video/Audio/File/Book, respectively. You can tell what kind of material is available by the icon next to the Free button. Sometimes you have to buy a course's books, but you can listen to the lectures for free.

7. Tap Get Course or Get Video/Audio/File/Book.

8. Tap the Library button at the top of the screen.

9. Tap iBooks to read any course books. Or, tap Videos in iTunes U to watch a video. (You also can get to videos by tapping Videos on the Home screen.)

10. Tap the icons on the bookshelf to view the course materials. Some courses provide a syllabus and a place to take notes. See Figure 11-14.

tech tip

To rearrange the icons on the iTunes U shelf, touch and hold an icon until it gets a bit bigger, and then drag it to a new position.

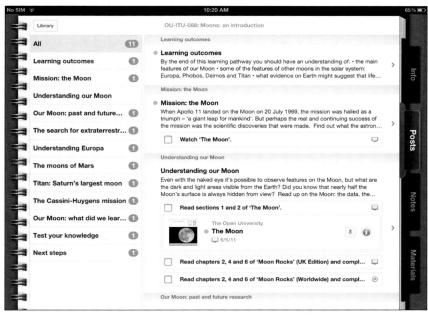

Figure 11-14

Chapter 12

Playing Music, Videos, and More

After you buy music, movies, and TV shows, you want to enjoy them. You know — play them! Media is divided by type on your iPad, so there's an app called Music that enables you to listen to music and spoken-word recordings (such as audio podcasts). Use the Videos app to watch visual media — movies, TV shows, video podcasts, and iTunes U videos.

YouTube is another media app that came with your iPad. YouTube is a collection of home movies and television clips from around the world by amateur and professional videographers alike. You can even upload your videos if you set up a YouTube account.

tech to connect

activities

- Choosing What to Listen To
- Controlling Music, Audiobooks, and Podcasts
- Making Playlists
- Turning On Closed Captioning
- Choosing What to Watch
- Controlling Videos and Movies
- Tuning In to YouTube
- Creating a YouTube Account
- Putting a Video on YouTube

Because you can store and play so many types of media on your iPad, it may become your preferred entertainment center. This chapter shows you how each app is set up and how to use the controls. The last tasks explain how to watch videos on YouTube, how to create a YouTube account, and then how to upload a video you take with your iPad on to your YouTube account so you can share it with your friends and family.

Choosing What to Listen To

If you like to listen to music, audiobooks, or podcasts, Music is the app for you. You can listen via the built-in speaker, by plugging your headphones or external speakers into the headphone port, or by docking your iPad in a speaker unit. (Refer to the "Plug it in" sidebar for more information.) However you listen, you'll see buttons across the bottom of the Music app screen:

- *Playlists* are groups of songs or podcasts that you put together as you like — a mixed tape, if you will. You can group playlists by musical style, the songs you recently added, and those recently played. Music comes with a few playlists already created, such as the 90s Music playlist. "Making Playlists" in this chapter explains how to create playlists. Figure 12-1 shows the Playlists view.
- *Songs* displays a list of all the music on your iPad sorted by song title.
- *Artists* shows small images of the artists whose music you have on your iPad.
- *Albums* shows all the albums you have on your iPad. Even if you downloaded just one song from an album on iTunes, the album cover appears here.
- *More* shows other views (such as Genres).

To play a song from the Music app, follow these steps:

1. Tap Music on the Home screen. The screen opens and looks a lot like what you see in Figure 12-1.

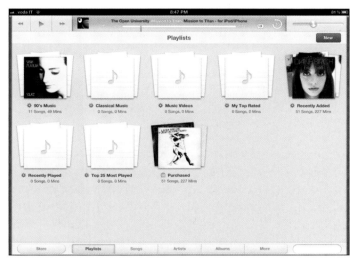

Figure 12-1

2. Tap Songs, Artists, or Albums.
3. Use these methods to find what you want to hear:
   - Tap the index on the right to go directly to the letter that the song, artist, or album name begins with.
   - Tap an artist to see a list of songs.
   - Tap an album to see the songs on that album.
4. Tap a song to play it. You can see my choice in Figure 12-2. When the song finishes, the next song in the list starts.

To play a podcast, audiobook, or iTunes U item, follow these steps:

1. Tap Music on the Home screen.
2. Tap More. You'll see the box shown in Figure 12-3.

3. Tap Podcasts, Audiobooks, or iTunes U.

4. Tap the icon that corresponds to the audio you want to hear.

5. Tap the track you want to hear from the list.

iTunes U media can be played from the iTunes U app too.

Figure 12-2   Figure 12-3

Controlling Music, Audiobooks, and Podcasts

When you tap a song, podcast, or audiobook, it begins playing immediately. The playback controls appear at the top of the screen, as shown in Figure 12-4. Refer to the figure to understand each of the following controls:

- Tap Previous/Rewind to start the song over. Tap it again to go to the previous track.
- Tap Play/Pause to pause the track. Tap it again to resume playing.
- Tap the Next/Fast Forward button to go to the next track. Hold the button to fast forward two seconds at a time.

Previous/Rewind
Play/Pause
Next/Fast Forward
Now Playing
Repeat
Playhead
Shuffle
Volume slider

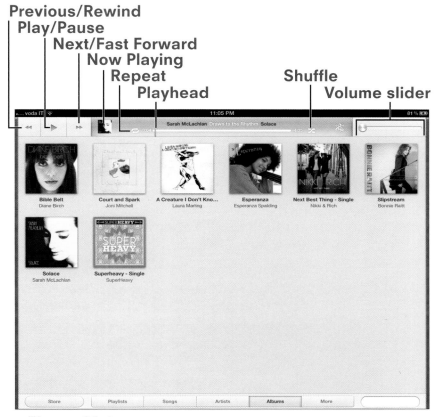

Figure 12-4

- For music only: Tap the Repeat button once to repeat all the songs on the album. Tap a second time to repeat the current song. Tap a third time to cancel repeating. For podcasts, audiobooks, and iTunes U: Tap the Repeat button to repeat the last 30 seconds of the audio. See Figure 12-5.

- Tap and drag the playhead (the red line) to go forward or backward within the currently playing audio.

- For music only: Tap the Shuffle button to play an album's songs in random order.

- Drag the Volume slider right or left to turn sound up or down.

- Tap the Now Playing icon to view the Now Playing screen. Tap the screen to see the controls again. Tap the Track List button (bottom right) to see the tracks. Tap the Back arrow in the lower left to return to the Music library view.

- For podcasts, audiobooks, or iTunes U: Tap the Playback Speed button once to play twice as fast; tap it again to play half as fast; tap it a third time to play at normal speed.

If you're using another app while you're listening to the Music app, double-click the Home button to see the Open Apps bar. Flick from left to right to reveal the playback controls shown in Figure 12-6. If you double-click the Home button when the iPad is locked, you see playback controls at the top of the screen. The buttons have the same functions as they do in the Music app.

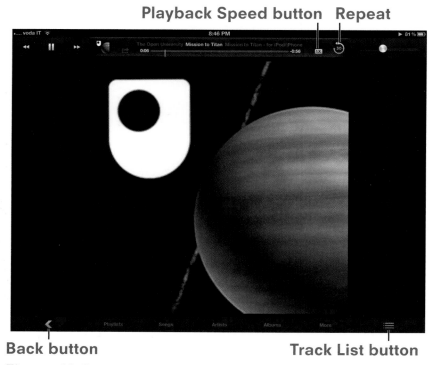

Figure 12-5

Plug it in

You can buy headphones, sometimes referred to as a headset or earphones or earbuds, to listen to audio on your iPad. When you plug them into the Headphone port, sound doesn't come out of the iPad speaker. Some headphones, such as Apple headphones, let you control playback with buttons on the cord. Additionally, you can purchase external speakers that you can either plug into your iPad's Headphone port or attach to the iPad via the Dock Connector.

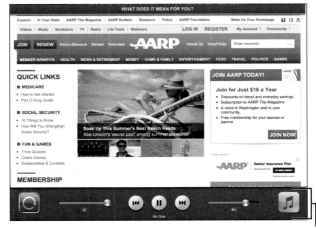

Playback controls

Figure 12-6

Making Playlists

A playlist is a mix of songs that you pull together from different albums and artists. The Music app includes some playlists to help you get started. You find playlists for the Most Recently Played songs and Recently Purchased. These so-called *smart playlists*, which automatically fill up with, respectively, the songs you listened to most recently and those you bought recently. Another included smart playlist is the 90s playlist, which recognizes songs from the 90s and adds them to that playlist.

To create your own playlist, follow these steps:

1. Tap Music on the Home screen.
2. Tap Playlists at the bottom.
3. Tap the New button at the top right.
4. Tap in the Title field.
5. Type a name for your playlist.
6. Tap Save.
7. Tap the songs you want in your playlist.
8. Tap Done when you've created a playlist you like. Your playlist appears on the screen. Mine is shown in Figure 12-7.
9. *Optional:* At any time, even after you listen to a playlist, tap the Edit button to do one of the following:
   - Delete songs. (Maybe one doesn't fit in with the playlist.)
   - Add more songs. The songs list opens and you can select songs.
10. Tap Done when you finish editing the playlist.
11. Play your playlist from the Playlists view as explained in this chapter's "Controlling Music, Audiobooks, and Podcasts."

If you ever want to delete an entire playlist, follow these steps:

1. Tap Music on the Home screen.
2. Tap Playlists.
3. Tap and hold for a few seconds on the playlist you want to delete.
4. When the X appears in the upper left, tap it. The music stays on your iPad, but the mix is deleted.

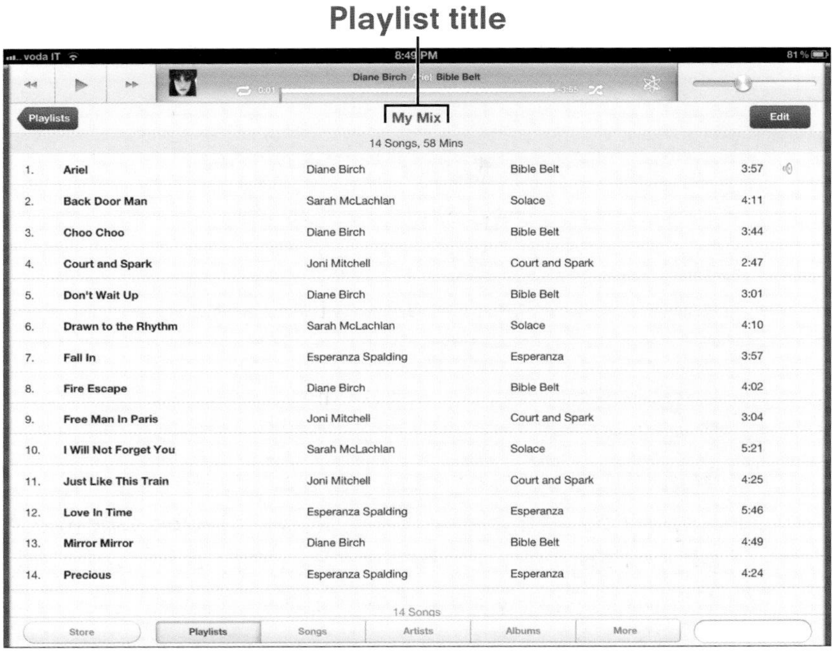

Playlist title

Figure 12-7

Turning On Closed Captioning

If you watch programs that offer closed captioning, here's a feature you may find helpful. Closed captioning is like subtitling: the audio portion is displayed as text on the screen.

Turn on closed captioning in the Videos app by following these steps:

1. Tap Settings on the Home screen.
2. Tap Videos in the Settings list.
3. Tap On for Closed Captioning, as shown in Figure 12-8.

Figure 12-8

Choosing What to Watch

You use the Videos app to watch videos that you've put on your iPad. Even when you download something from iTunes U, you can watch it in Videos. The app categorizes by type: Movies, TV Shows, Podcasts, and iTunes U.

Turn your iPad sideways to see if viewing is improved.

To watch a video, take the following steps:

1. Tap Videos on the Home screen.
2. Tap an option:
   - Movies
   - Rentals
   - TV Shows
   - Podcasts
   - iTunes U

You only see tabs for the type of video you have, which means you won't see Movie or Rentals tabs if you haven't downloaded any movies.

3. Tap the icon for the movie, show, or podcast you want to watch. The icon unfolds and the movie screen opens, as shown in Figure 12-9. Figure 12-10 shows a podcast screen.

4. Tap the Play button. For a movie, you can tap a specific chapter. For a TV show or podcast, you can tap the episode.

Before you start watching, you can tap these options:

- Tap the Info button at the top to read a description of the movie or series.

- Tap the More button (TV Shows, Podcasts, iTunes U) next to the episode to read a longer description of that episode.

- Tap Get More Episodes (TV Shows, Podcasts, iTunes U) to open that series in the iTunes Store. Then you can buy and download additional episodes.

- Tap the button in the upper left to return to the media library from the iTunes Store. What the button says depends on what you're watching.

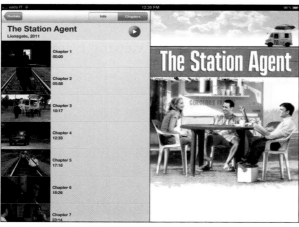

Figure 12-9

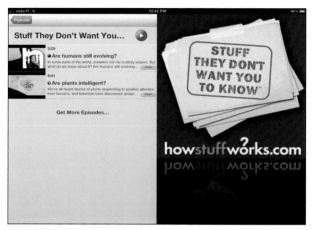

Figure 12-10

Controlling Videos and Movies

You can just let the video go, but you may want to adjust some options, like the volume (if it's too low) or aspect ratio (if it's distorted). You may want to rewind or fast forward to re-watch or skip parts of the video.

Follow these steps to watch your video and make adjustments:

- Tap the video you want to watch. It fills the screen, as shown in Figure 12-11.
- Tap the Play/Pause button to pause the video. Tap again to resume playing.
- Tap Rewind once to return to the beginning of the episode. Tap twice to go back one chapter (scene) in a movie or to go to a previous episode of a series. Touch and hold to rewind.
- Tap Fast Forward to go to the next chapter in a movie. Tap and hold to fast forward quickly through the movie.

Figure 12-11

- Drag the white ball, known as the *playhead*, right or left to move forward and backward in the video. Slide your finger down as you drag the playhead to adjust the speed at which the video moves. The time on the left is the time the video has played; the time on the right is the time remaining.

- Tap the Fill/Fit button to toggle between two ways you can view video.

- For movies that have subtitle or language options, tap a button that looks like a dialog bubble to see your options.

- Tap Done when you want to stop watching and return to the info screen. Or, press the Home button. If you stop watching before a video is finished, it later picks up playing where you left off.

The Search field is available in both the Music and Videos apps. Tap in the Search field to bring up the keyboard and then type what you want to search for (such as song name, artist, or show title). As always, the more letters you type, the narrower your search results.

Tuning In to YouTube

YouTube is a website where anyone and everyone can upload video, and anyone and everyone can watch the videos. You find a little bit — and sometimes a lot — of everything on YouTube: home movies, funny animals, episodes of old television shows (I'm particularly fond of *Bewitched*), clips from current shows, news, movie trailers, how-to videos for fitness, home repair, shopping guides, and about anything else you can think of.

The difference between YouTube and Videos is that you don't download YouTube videos. When you watch a video on YouTube, you are *streaming* the video (that is, watching it online). That means you must have a cellular or Wi-Fi connection to watch anything on YouTube. If you have a Wi-Fi connection, the image streams quickly. If you have a cellular connection, such as 3G or 4G, you see the YouTube logo as the video loads. It will begin playing after enough of the video has begun streaming. A word of caution, however: Streaming video via cellular can quickly eat up your cellular data allotment. If you exceed your limit, you must pay extra or risk not having any cellular data services until the next month begins.

The videos you see in any of the lists (refer to Figure 12-12) have the same information:

- Video image
- Video name
- Rating (Percentage of all the people who voted either Like or Dislike for the video)
- Views (Total number of times the video has been watched)
- Time (How long the video runs)
- Author (Username of the person who posted the video)

Here's how to have some fun on YouTube:

1. Tap YouTube on the Home screen. A screen similar to the one shown in Figure 12-12 appears.

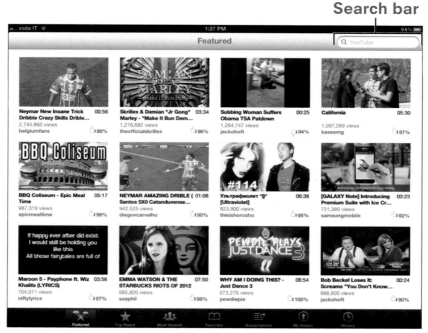

Figure 12-12

2. Tap in the Search bar and type something you're interested in. Or, tap one of the buttons at the bottom of the screen:

   ▪ *Featured* displays a list of videos selected by the YouTube editors.

   ▪ *Top Rated* are based on viewers liking or disliking the video. (They do that by tapping on an icon.) Tap the tabs at the top to see videos for today, this week, or in all of YouTube history.

   ▪ *Most Viewed* shows the most watched videos. Tap the tabs to see the most-viewed videos for today, this week, or in all of YouTube history.

3. Tap the video image to start it. Tap the buttons that are pointed out in Figure 12-13 to control the video.

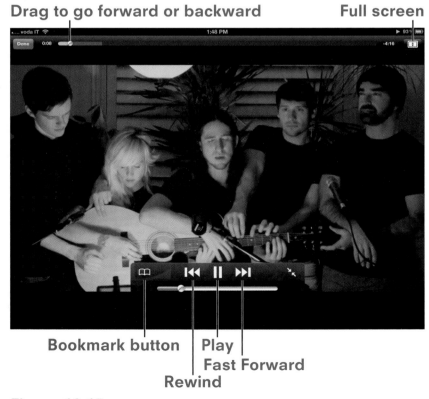

Drag to go forward or backward   **Full screen**

Bookmark button   **Play**
                      Fast Forward
          Rewind

Figure 12-13

4. *Optional:* Tap the Bookmark button to add the video to your Favorites list.

5. Tap Done or the Full-Screen toggle button to stop watching. The viewing screen gets smaller and a list of other videos runs down the right side of the screen, as shown in Figure 12-14.

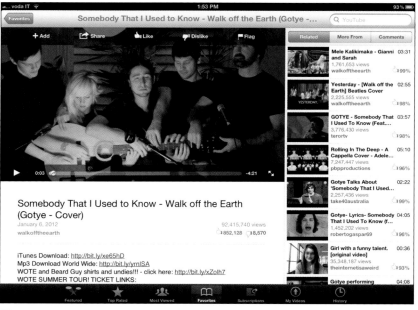

Figure 12-14

6. *Optional:* Tap a button to do the following:

   ▪ *Add* (+) lets you add this video to your Favorites or to a playlist, if you've created any.

   ▪ *Share* lets you send a link to this video to someone via Mail. The Mail app opens when you tap this button. A new message is ready to be addressed and sent.

   ▪ *Like/Dislike* adds your vote to the video. You must have a YouTube account to do this.

   ▪ *Flag* means you think the material violates the YouTube Community Guidelines. Such material includes pornography or graphic violence.

7. *Optional:* When the video is finished, tap a tab (above the column on the right):

   ■ *Related* lists videos that are similar to the one you just watched.

   ■ *More From* shows videos on YouTube from the same author.

   ■ *Comments* lists comments written by others about this video. If you have an account, you can add your own comment.

The main YouTube screen offers other tabs as well:

■ *Favorites* lists videos you've marked as your favorites. Add videos to this list by tapping the Bookmark button while the video is open. You can also create playlists from this screen.

■ *Subscriptions* shows the channels or users you've subscribed to. You can subscribe if you want to be notified when a specific user posts a new video. Find a video you like, tap the More From tab, and then tap the Subscribe button.

■ *My Videos* lists videos that you've uploaded to YouTube.

■ *History* shows the videos that you've watched.

Creating a YouTube Account

Signing up for a YouTube account is completely optional. You don't need a YouTube account to watch videos on YouTube.

If you want to post videos of your own, subscribe to another account, or rate videos, you must have an account with YouTube. If you have a Gmail account, you can sign in with your Gmail e-mail address and password. (Google owns YouTube.)

Create a YouTube account by following these steps:

1. Tap Safari on the Home screen.
2. Tap in the URL field.
3. Type `youtube.com`.
4. Scroll down the screen and tap Sign In.
5. Tap Sign Up For YouTube! The screen as shown in Figure 12-15 opens.

Figure 12-15

6. Tap in the Name fields and type your name.
7. Tap in the Choose a Google Username field.
8. Type a username. This is the name everyone on YouTube sees when you comment or post videos. You can use your name or choose something a bit more anonymous and clever.

9. Tap in Create a Password and type a password.

10. Tap in Confirm Your Password and type your password again.

11. Tap Month, Day, and Year and add your birth date. YouTube confirms your legal age because you must be 13 or older to post videos to YouTube and over 18 to watch certain videos. You can hide your age in the Personal Details of the Profile Setup part of My Account.

12. *Optional:* You don't have to answer these questions: Gender, Mobile Phone, Other E-Mail Address, and Location.

13. Tap in the Type the Two Pieces of Text box. Type the words (one of which will be distorted). If you can't decipher what's written, tap the reload button to see a new choice. If you prefer to hear it, tap the speaker button. If you want more information, tap the question mark.

14. Read the terms of service and privacy policy.

15. Tap the box next to I Agree to the Google Terms of Service and Privacy Policy. If you don't agree, you can't create an account.

16. Tap the box that says Google May Use My Account Information. Make sure it *does not* have a check mark. This is a small step that can help protect your privacy.

17. Tap Next Step.

18. Sign in to your account by typing your username and e-mail address.

Putting a Video on YouTube

You might have seen some funny videos on YouTube made by people like yourself. You may be thinking that you'd like to put some of your own videos on YouTube. Chapter 8 explains how to make video with your iPad and watch it there. After you create a YouTube account, you can share your video on YouTube as well. Videos should be 15 minutes or less, although users in good standing can request the privilege to upload longer videos.

Follow these steps to upload your video to YouTube and then send an e-mail to your friends and family so they can see what you created:

1. Tap Photos on the Home screen.
2. Tap the Photos tab at the top.
3. Tap the video you want to send to YouTube.
4. Tap the Share button in the upper right. Figure 12-16 shows the choices that come up.
5. Tap Send to YouTube. A window asks for your YouTube name and password.
6. Type in your YouTube name and password.
7. Tap Sign In. The Publish Video window appears, as shown in Figure 12-17.

Figure 12-16   Figure 12-17

8. Tap in each field and type in the required information.
9. Tap an option:
   - Standard Definition looks just fine on a small device like an iPad or iPod.

■ HD creates a bigger file, which takes longer to upload and view.

10. Tap Tags.

11. Type single words that define your video. If someone searches for a word that is one of your tags, your video appears in the search results (if your video is set to Public, as explained in step 13).

12. Tap Category and tap an option.

tech tip

13. Tap Public, Unlisted, or Private to determine who can view your video. Consider your privacy carefully before making the video Public.

14. Tap Publish. Your video is sent to YouTube.

You can watch your video on YouTube as well:

1. Press the Home button on the iPad frame.

2. Tap the YouTube app icon.

3. Tap My Videos to view your video.

4. *Optional:* Tap the Share button to send an e-mail to people.

To see more YouTube settings options, you have to go to the YouTube website from Safari. Here you can change the privacy settings or disable comments. Follow these steps:

1. Tap Safari on the Home screen.

2. Tap in the URL field.

3. Type youtube.com.

4. Tap Sign In.

5. Tap in the correct fields and type your YouTube username and password.

6. Tap the Sign In button.

7. Tap My Channel in the list toward the left.

8. Tap Video Manager in the upper right.

9. Tap the Edit button next to the video whose settings you want to change.

10. Tap Advanced Settings.

11. Change the Comments choices as you wish.

Chapter 13

Taking Notes and Making Lists

No matter what your age, you have undoubtedly had trouble remembering everything you want to remember. Whether it's things to do or ideas that I have, my brain seems to go on overload after a certain hour of the day or a certain number — like more than two — of items to recall. Now you can keep track of everything in one place: your portable iPad. This chapter explains how to use two apps that can help: Notes and Reminders.

In Notes you *jot* things down. I use Notes to make my grocery list, to record titles of books I want to read, and to write paragraphs for present and future projects I'm working on. Here I show you how to create notes and go back to read or edit them later. I also explain how to send a note from Notes via e-mail.

I use Reminders to make to-do lists. Here, too, you can create as many lists as long as you like. Reminders is great for organizing related tasks in one list and then having a different list for each project or topic. For example, if you are organizing a vacation, you could make a list in Reminders named Vacation and list the tasks you need to do, such as renew passport, make airline and hotel reservations, suspend the newspaper delivery, and so on. I describe how to add tasks to a list and how to create multiple lists. The last two tasks focus on adding a timed reminder to specific tasks and setting the alert tone and style for the timed reminders you create.

Creating and Viewing Notes

If you're a list maker like me, you'll find yourself turning to the Notes app again and again. It's simple to use, and I like the yellow legal pad graphic and the lack of wasted paper. There's no limit to the number of notes you write nor the length of each note.

If you have a Wi-Fi connection, you can speak your notes instead of typing them. Tap the dictation key on the keyboard, speak your note, and tap the dictation key again. The text you dictated appears on the note. The dictation key is pointed out in Figure 13-1.

To create notes and then move from one to another, do the following:

1. Tap Notes on the Home screen.
2. Tap anywhere on the yellow "paper."
3. Type your note. You can see my grocery list in Figure 13-1. The first line is also the title of the note, so you might want to type something like *Groceries* or *Books to Read* or *Gift Ideas* on the first line.
4. Tap the note page.

Add Note button

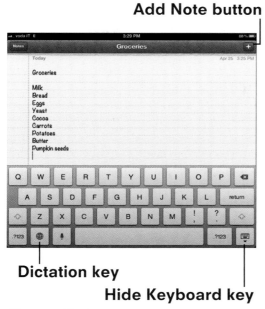

Dictation key

Hide Keyboard key

Figure 13-1

When you're in Notes, you can also use these moves:

- *Make the keyboard disappear:* Tap the Hide Keyboard key.
- *Add another note:* Tap the Add Note button (plus symbol) in the upper right.
- *See all your notes:* They're arranged chronologically, with the most recently created or edited at the top of the list. The active, or open, note is circled in the list. Do one of the following:
  - Turn your iPad to landscape view so the Notes list and the active note appear side by side. See Figure 13-2.
  - Turn your iPad to portrait view. Tap the Notes button in the upper left.
- *Move from one note to another:* Do one of the following:
  - In the Notes list, tap the note you want to read or edit.
  - In a note, tap the Previous or Next button.
- *Edit your note:* Use the same gestures and commands you use in an e-mail, which is explained in Chapter 3. You can,

for example, copy and paste text from one note or message into a different note or message.

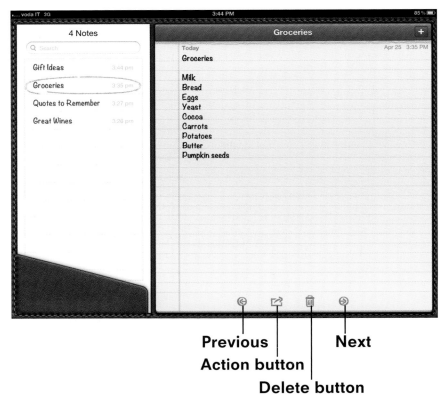

Figure 13-2

Sending, Printing, or Deleting a Note

If you write a great note, you may want to share it with someone else. You can either send it as an e-mail or print it. On the other hand, you will want to get rid of other notes (old shopping lists, for example). In that case, in the Notes list, just tap the Delete (trashcan) button.

To send a note via e-mail, take these steps:

1. In the Notes list, tap the note you want to send.
2. Tap the Action button (rectangle with arrow). The button is pointed out in Figure 13-2.
3. Tap Email to create an e-mail message that has your note. Figure 13-3 shows such a message.
4. Tap in the To field.

Tap to add recipients

| Cancel | Groceries | Send |

To: ⊕

Cc/Bcc:

Subject: Groceries

Groceries

Milk
Bread
Eggs
Yeast
Cocoa
Carrots
Potatoes
Butter

Figure 13-3

5. Type the intended recipient (and it may very well be yourself). A list of suggested recipients saved in Contacts appears.
6. Tap the intended recipient. Or, type the entire e-mail address if it isn't one you have saved in Contacts.
7. Tap in the Subject field and type.
8. *Optional:* Tap in the message body and type.
9. Tap Send.

To print a note, follow these steps:

1. In the Notes list, tap the note you want to send.
2. Tap the Action button (rectangle with arrow). The button is pointed out in Figure 13-2.
3. Tap Print.
4. Tap the Printer button. There must be an AirPrint-compatible printer on the same Wi-Fi network to which your iPad is connected. (Or you must have AirPrint Activator 2 or Printopia on your computer to make shared printers accessible via AirPrint.)
5. Tap the plus sign to indicate the number of copies you want to print.
6. Tap the Print button.

Changing the Notes Font

You have three choices for the typeface, or font, used to write your notes:

- *Noteworthy* is the font shown in this chapter's figures.
- *Helvetica* is a very clean, traditional typeface.
- *Marker Felt* uses letters that are a little thicker than Noteworthy; they look like they're written with a fine-tipped marker.

When you change font, the text in *all* your notes and the Notes list changes. To change the font, do the following:

1. Tap Settings on the Home screen.
2. Tap Notes in the Settings list. The Notes settings appear, as shown in Figure 13-4.

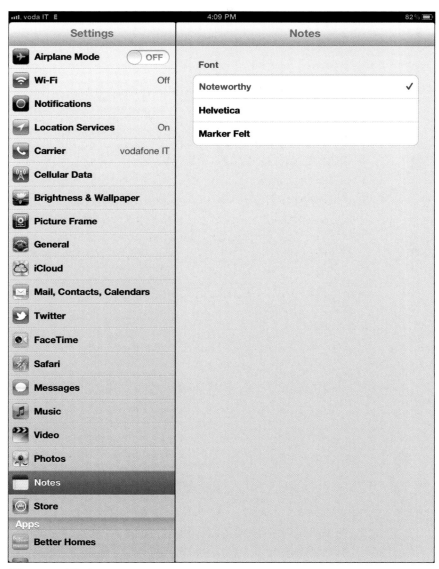

Figure 13-4

3. Tap the font you prefer.

4. Tap the home button to return to the Home screen.

Making and Editing Lists in Reminders

If you have a later-generation iPad, you can use the Reminders app to create simple checklists. You can create different checklists for different types of tasks, such as *Spring Cleaning To Dos* or *Garage Sale To Dos*. Then, check off each item as you complete it, and the item is moved to a list titled Completed. The Reminders app comes with two lists: Reminders and Completed.

Follow these steps to put tasks on the Reminders list:

1. Tap Reminders on the Home screen.

2. Tap the piece of "paper." Or, tap the plus symbol in the upper right.

3. Type the task you want to remember. The task appears in the list with a check box to the left.

4. Tap the Return key.

5. Repeat steps 2–4 to add more tasks.

6. Tap the home button to leave Reminders when you finish creating your list.

tech tip

You can change an existing reminder, and you'll definitely want to mark it as completed if you are done.

1. Tap Reminders on the Home screen.

2. Tap the reminder (on the left) that has the task(s) you want to mark complete.

3. In the list on the right, tap the check box next to a task you have completed. You can see the check boxes in Figure 13-5.

Tap the Completed list to see the tasks that you have accomplished (and marked thusly) from every list. Each list has its own Completed section, which you view by scrolling up the list. Tapping to take the check mark *off* an item in the Completed list moves it back to its original list.

To keep the task on the list, but change its wording, do this:

1. Tap Reminders on the Home screen.
2. Tap the reminder (on the left) that has the task(s) you want to mark complete or edit.
3. Tap the task you want to edit (on the right) to open the Details window.
4. Tap in the Task field.
5. Tap and hold text to select.
6. Do one of the following:
   - Type new text.
   - Copy, cut, and paste from Reminders to another app (or from another app to Reminders).

Tap to see all completed tasks

Tap to send to Completed   **Tap to type**

voda IT 3G	5:32 PM	73%
Edit List Date	Reminders	+
Q Search Reminders	1 Completed	
Completed	☑ Pick up dry cleaning	
Reminders ✔	☐ Make dentist appointment	
	☐ Pick up prescription	
	☐ Call vet for Star's shots	

Figure 13-5

Adding or Deleting Lists in Reminders

The Reminders app comes with two lists: Reminders and Completed. You can add other lists and then add new reminders on the lists you create.

To rearrange the order of reminders, tap Edit. Then drag the List button to the right of the items.

To add a list, follow these steps:

1. Tap Reminders on the Home screen.
2. Tap the List tab (if you aren't in List view).
3. Tap the Edit button.
4. Tap Create New List, which you can see in Figure 13-6.
5. Type a list name.
6. Tap the Done key on the keyboard.

To delete a list, follow these steps:

1. Tap Reminders on the Home screen.
2. Tap the List button (if you aren't in List view).
3. Tap the Edit button.
4. Tap the Delete button (white minus symbol on red) to the left of the list name in the list. Figure 13-6 points out the Delete button.
5. Tap the Delete button that appears to the right of the list name.
6. Tap Delete to confirm.
7. Tap Done to return to the Reminders screen.
8. Tap the list you want to see or edit. It appears on the white "paper" on the right with a checkmark next to it in the list.

Delete button

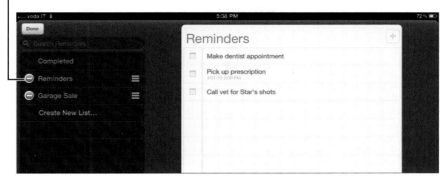

Figure 13-6

Setting Timed Reminders

You can get a reminder about your reminder. Assign a date and time for when you want an alert. If the task repeats, you can set up Reminders to automatically remind you in the future as well.

Do the following to add a Remind Me alert to an item on a Reminders list:

1. Tap Reminders on the Home screen.
2. Tap the List tab (if you aren't in List view).
3. Tap the list that contains the task.
4. Tap the task you want Reminders to help you remember. The Details screen opens, as shown in Figure 13-7.
5. Tap Show More.
6. Tap Remind Me.
7. Tap On for the On A Day option.
8. Tap the date that appears. A date and time rotor opens, as shown in Figure 13-8.

9. Scroll through the date and time to set when you want to be reminded of this task.

10. Tap Done. The date and time appear in the Remind Me field.

11. Tap Repeat if your event happens regularly.

12. Tap an option:
    - None
    - Every Day
    - Every Week
    - Every 2 Weeks
    - Every Month
    - Every Year

For example, if you want to update the software on your iPad every month, tap Monthly. Remember that Every Week or Every Two Weeks will send a reminder on the same day of the week. For example, you'll get an alert every Friday; Every Month will alert you to the task on the same date every month, such as April 27, May 27, June 27, and so on.

13. Tap Done.

14. *Optional:* Tap Priority and tap an option:
    - Low
    - Medium
    - High

15. Tap Done.

16. *Optional:* Tap Notes and type information about this task.

17. Tap Done to close the Details window.

If you add a timed reminder to lots of tasks, it can be helpful to view all the tasks for one day. Tap the Date tab and then tap the day for which you want to view tasks.

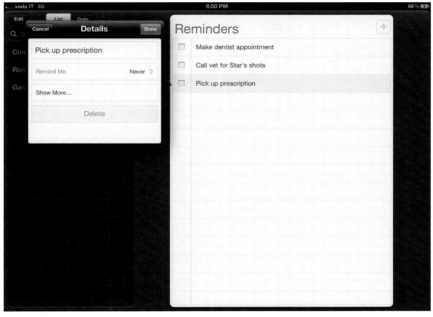

Figure 13-7

Figure 13-8

Choosing the Reminder Alert Style

I talk about alerts and the Notification Center in Chapter 2 but think it needs a special mention here. You can choose how you want Reminders to remind you of the task you asked for a reminder for. Now there's a tongue twister for you!

I recommend choosing alerts instead of a banner. Banners are more easily missed.

Follow these steps to set up Reminder notifications:

1. Tap Settings on the Home screen.
2. Tap Notifications in the Settings list.
3. Tap Reminders in the Notifications settings window. The Reminders screen appears, as shown in Figure 13-9.
4. Tap On for the Notification Center option. Your reminders will be listed in the Notification Center. You can see the Center by dragging your finger down from the top of the iPad screen towards the center.
5. Tap an option for Alert Style:

   - *None* means a nonvisual alert will appear when a reminder comes due. You can still set a sound alert by following steps 6 through 9.
   - *Banners* appear at the top of the screen for a few seconds and then disappear.
   - *Alerts* make you tap something before you can do anything else on your iPad.

6. Tap General in the Settings list.
7. Tap Sounds in the General settings window.
8. Tap Reminder Alerts in the Sounds settings.
9. In the Reminder Alerts list, tap the alert tone you want to hear when Reminders reminds you of a timed task. Figure 13-10 shows some of your options.

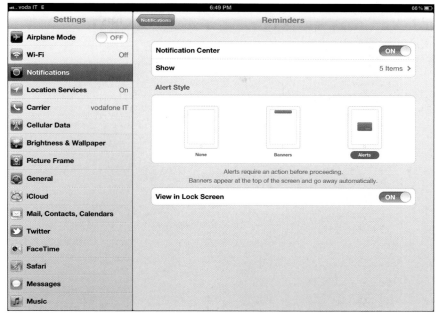

Figure 13-9

Figure 13-10

Chapter 14

Heading Off Trouble

No one likes to admit it, but problems with electronic devices usually have more to do with the user than the device itself. Take my printer, for example. Frequently, seemingly out of the blue, it doesn't work. Time after time I discover I've hit the plug with the vacuum cleaner — not enough to unplug it completely, but dislodged just enough to interrupt the contact. It looks like it's plugged in, but when I push in the plug slightly more, it works perfectly.

tech to connect

activities

- **Keeping Your Software Up-to-Date**
- **Troubleshooting a Wi-Fi Connection**
- **Troubleshooting a Cellular Connection**
- **Troubleshooting Messages and E-Mail**
- **Troubleshooting On/Off Functions**
- **Troubleshooting Apps**
- **Contacting Apple Support**

iPads can be like that too. All of a sudden something you do every day doesn't work. Before packing it up and taking it to the Apple store (or waiting on hold to talk to a technical support person), try going through the steps in this chapter. You'll have a great sense of satisfaction when it works, and if it doesn't, you'll know you tried everything you could. What constitutes a problem on your iPad? Maybe the screen goes black; or tapping, swiping, and scrolling have no effect. Look through this list to find the problem you have and then try the steps.

The first tasks in this chapter take you through steps that can help fix common problems. The next task confronts slightly more complicated problems. Another task explains how to contact Apple customer support and what to expect from them.

Keeping Your Software Up-to-Date

Like a computer or smartphone, your iPad is a mix of hardware — the physical case and circuits inside — and software — the operating system (the instructions the circuits follow) and apps (smaller instructions for doing specific tasks). Keeping the operating system software on your iPad up-to-date is an easy way to avoid problems. Apple works constantly to improve the operating system and iron out kinks that come up. When an operating system update is available, you see a badge on the Settings button on the Home screen.

To see if new software is available, and to download it, do the following:

1. Tap Settings on the Home screen.

2. Tap General in the Settings list.

3. Tap Software Update in the General list, as shown in Figure 14-1. The Software Update says *Checking for Update.* If an update is available, it is automatically installed on your iPad.

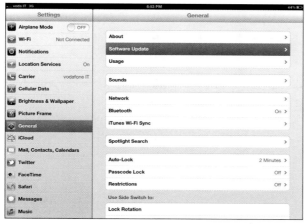

Figure 14-1

Troubleshooting a Wi-Fi Connection

If you try to visit the Internet in Safari or check your e-mail in Mail and receive a message like the one shown in Figure 14-2, you don't have an Internet connection. The first thing to check is your Wi-Fi connection. Sometimes, you don't have Wi-Fi access simply because it's turned off. Follow these steps to check:

1. Tap Settings on the Home screen.

2. Tap Off for the Wi-Fi option.

3. Wait a minute or two.

4. Tap On for the Wi-Fi option.

If Wi-Fi is on but you still can't connect, try this:

1. Tap Settings on the Home screen.
2. Tap General.
3. Tap Reset Network Settings.

Figure 14-2

Troubleshooting a Cellular Connection

If you have a Wi-Fi iPad, you can skip this section. To understand the difference between Wi-Fi and cellular data, think of Wi-Fi as using a landline (a phone plugged into the wall) versus cellular as using a mobile phone (a cellphone).

If you see the words *No Service* where your carrier's name usually appears, these steps are for you. (This applies only to 3G/4G iPads with a SIM card.) If none of these tactics works, contact your cellular service provider.

1. Tap Settings on the Home screen.
2. Tap On for the Airplane Mode setting.
3. Move your body:
   - Closer to a window
   - Outside
   - Away from running microwaves
   - Away from cordless base phone stations
4. Turn your iPad off and then back on.

5. Gently use the SIM Removal Tool to open the SIM tray by inserting the point into the small hole above the SIM tray door. See Figure 14-3.

6. Gently lift the SIM card out of the tray.

7. Re-insert the SIM card, making sure it's in the direction indicated on the tray.

8. Push the SIM tray closed.

If that doesn't work, try this:

1. Tap Settings on the Home screen.

2. Tap General.

3. Tap Reset Network Settings.

You know you have Wi-Fi access when you see the Wi-Fi icon in the status bar at the top of the iPad screen, as in Figure 14-4. It looks like a fan with three stripes. The more stripes you see in black, the stronger the Wi-Fi signal. If you have a 3G/4G iPad, you also see the cellular connection icon as indicated.

—SIM card

Photo courtesy Heather Funk
Figure 14-3

Cellular connection   **Wi-Fi connection**

Figure 14-4

Troubleshooting Messages and E-Mail

You can't send messages from Messages.

1. Look at the status bar and make sure you have cellular or Wi-Fi service. Refer back to Figure 14-4. If you don't, follow the steps in "Troubleshooting a Wi-Fi Connection" in this chapter.
2. Check that the recipient's e-mail address (or phone number) is typed in correctly.

You can't receive or send e-mail.

1. Look at the status bar and make sure you have cellular or Wi-Fi service. If not, follow the first steps outlined previously.
2. Tap Settings on the Home screen.
3. Tap Mail, Contacts, Calendars.
4. Tap Account Name.
5. Tap Account.
6. Delete and retype your password.

You can't hear anything but your headset is plugged in. What to do? Make sure the headset is plugged in all the way. It makes a little click when it's all the way in.

Troubleshooting On/Off Functions

Some common problems are a little more difficult to fix.

Your iPad won't turn on.

1. Connect your iPad to the USB connector cable and power adapter to begin charging. See Figure 14-5.
2. When you see the Apple logo onscreen, turn on your iPad.

Attach the USB connector...
     to the power adapter   **Then plug this end into the iPad**

Figure 14-5

Troubleshooting Apps

An app has frozen on your screen, and pressing the Home button doesn't do anything.

1. Hold down the Sleep/Wake switch until the Slide to Power Off message appears. The Sleep/Wake switch is on the top right of the iPad frame when it's in portrait mode.
2. Hold the home button (on the front of the iPad's frame) until the frozen app quits.
3. Tap the feisty app on the Home screen to see if it opens normally.

If that doesn't work, try this:

1. Hold down the home button and the Sleep/Wake switch simultaneously for about 10 seconds.
2. Release when you see the Apple logo onscreen. When your iPad restarts, it should work properly.

The same app keeps giving you trouble:

1. Tap and hold the app on the Home screen until all the apps wiggle.
2. Tap the X in the upper-left corner of the troublesome app. This deletes the app.
3. Tap the home button on the iPad's frame.
4. Tap the App Store icon on the Home screen.
5. Tap the Purchased button at the bottom of the screen.
6. Tap the app to re-install it.

The problems still occur or occur with more than one app:

1. Tap Settings on the Home screen.
2. Tap General.
3. Tap Reset.
4. Tap Reset All Settings.
5. Redo the settings you changed since you started using your iPad, such as alerts, screen orientation, or wallpaper.

You tried all of the previous solutions but things still aren't quite right. Try this:

1. Tap Settings on the Home screen.
2. Tap iCloud.
3. Tap Storage & Backup.
4. Tap Backup Now.
5. Tap General in the Settings list.
6. Tap Reset.
7. Tap Erase All Content and Settings.
8. Go through the iPad setup explained in Chapter 1.
9. Tap Restore from iCloud Backup, as shown in Figure 14-6.

Figure 14-6

Accessing Apple Support

If you have a problem I didn't mention in this chapter, or none of the steps resolve your problem, you can find more help on the Internet. (But if your iPad is your only access to the web — you don't have a desktop computer, for instance — you'll have to ask to use a friend or relative's computer, or use a computer at a public library.)

Your first stop should be Apple's iPhone Support page at
`www.apple.com/support/ipad`. You can contact Apple's
technical support group for personal attention.

I have always found Apple's warranty and repair service to be
both efficient and professional. Your iPad includes a one-year
warranty, and you can buy a second year of coverage (called
AppleCare) any time within the first year of ownership.
Purchased AppleCare also adds extra "no-fault" insurance
during the first year. That means that if anything goes wrong
with your iPad — even if it's your fault: you drop it and the
screen shatters or you spill your coffee on it — you can call
Apple or take it to an Apple store for a repair or a replace-
ment. It's cheaper than buying a new iPad.

If possible, back everything up as explained in the online
bonus chapter, "Securing Your Data and iPad," before
you leave your iPad with Apple. That way, you can put everything (contacts, music, and so on) back on the repaired
iPad. The chapter is online at `www.wiley.com/go/`
`ipadtechtoconnect`.

Index